Jonathan Holden a Partner, Head of Employment and Head of Education for Forbes Solicitors. He has specialised in Employment Law throughout his career. Jonathan has extensive experience in advising public sector institutions; and is a nationally recognised expert in advising on employment law issues within the education sector.

He is an experienced Tribunal advocate, and regularly appears in Employment Tribunals throughout the country. He is experienced in dealing with pension loss issues, and appeared in one of the leading cases in this area in the Employment Appeals Tribunal. Jonathan is one of few experts nationally on LGPS and Teacher's Pension issues; and he is currently dealing with a Court of Appeal case dealing with gross misconduct in the Education sector. He commonly deals with complicated discrimination and whistle-blowing cases. In addition, he is experienced in dealing with both the non-contentious and contentious implications of the Transfer of Undertakings (Protection of Employment) Regulations and advises clients on these issues both internally, and at Tribunal if necessary.

In addition, Jonathan presents seminars to clients on all aspects of Employment Law and provides bespoke in-house training to meet client demand. He also regularly comments on Employment issues to local media and radio as well writing for and on the education sector; and has recently been retained by a national training provider to train lawyers on employment law issues within the education sector.

I0894823

A Practical Guide for School Business Leaders and Headteachers on Employment Law in Schools

A Practical Guide for School Business Leaders and Headteachers on Employment Law in Schools

Jonathan Holden, BA (Hons), PgDL
National Head of Education and Employment, Forbes Solicitors

Law Brief Publishing

Published 2019 by Law Brief Publishing, an imprint of Law Brief Publishing Ltd
30 The Parks
Minehead
Somerset
TA24 8BT

www.lawbriefpublishing.com

Paperback: 978-1-912687-43-5

For Rachel, always

PREFACE

Running a School is difficult. The time pressure alone is significant, to say nothing of having to manage the sometimes competing interests of stakeholders: be that parents, staff, trade unions, local authorities, OFSTED…

I hope this book will make the job just a little bit easier.

This book is not a comprehensive statement of the law. That would be a work worthy of a substantial number of volumes at the very least. What this book aims to do is to pick out areas and aspects of Employment law that have most impact and are (hopefully) to School Business Leaders and Headteachers in the day to day running of School. It is no substitute for legal advice, but does aim to make you more knowledgeable and to be an easy point of reference when a particular situation arises.

Whilst I hope to have covered most, if not all, areas of relevance, I am always interested to receive feedback on any aspect. I would be particularly interested to hear from School Business Leaders and Heads with feedback on any areas they would like covered either at all or in more detail in any future edition. To that end, email is simplest – jonathan.holden@forbessolicitors.co.uk.

At this stage, I would like to thank first my family, and my fantastic team at Forbes Solicitors for their support on putting this project together. Finally, I would like to thank all those Schools and clients who have formed the basis of my experience, enabling me to put a book like this together – and I can promise at this stage that none of your cases feature in the book!

The law is correct as at 1st October 2019. All errors are my own.

Jonathan Holden
October 2019

PREFACE

CONTENTS

CHAPTER ONE
WHO IS THE EMPLOYER?

Introduction

In this chapter, we will look at some of the considerations in determ-ining whether a person is employed, self-employed, or a worker; then look in more detail and the provisions in maintained Schools around appointment, suspension and dismissal.

Employee, Self-Employed or Worker

For the vast majority of time, those within School will be employees, working under a contract of employment with the School, Academy, or Local Authority. However, there are occasions where a School might engage with a 'casual' member of staff. There has been a huge amount of litigation over the years in this area; most recently centred around the gig economy, particularly the taxi app Uber.

You may ask why it matters: and the reason is all down to the rights granted to Employees, and those that can fit into the category of 'worker': who, whilst not employees, nevertheless are entitled to paid holidays, for example.

So how do you make a call in School between the different categories? The first thing to do is to look at any contractual documentation. If there is an Employment contract in place, the answer is straightforward. If it is a self-employment agreement (for example for a consultant), important points in favour of it being genuine self-employment include a right of substitution (i.e. the right to send another individual instead to do the work they are engaged to do), responsibility for tax resting with the individual, and from a practical point of view you should also check they have indemnity insurance.

Remember always that the trend in the Courts is to protect the rights of the individual, giving them 'worker' (if not Employee) rights. The Courts will go behind an Employment contract if it is a sham, and look at the position on the ground: if the Employer/Organisation retains a sufficient degree of control over the individual, they are likely to be classed at least as workers.

Types of School

There are a dizzying array of different Schools within the education landscape; but all can be categorised into three main types:

- Academies (including multi-academy trusts);
- Maintained Schools; and
- Independent Schools

Within Academies, MATs and Independent Schools, identifying the correct Employer is relatively straightforward: the Employer will be the Academy Trust, or the organisation by which the independent school is owned or run. It is important that the correct employer is stated on the contract of employment; note also that should this change for any reason, Employees must be sent notification of the change in writing. This can be done either by the issue of an updated contract, or by a side letter. The time limit for doing this is within one month of the change in question.

In a maintained School, the position as to who the correct Employer is can be confusing. If in any doubt, the quickest place to look is the latest OFSTED report which will confirm the type of School under the heading 'School Details'.

Type of School	Employer
Community	Local Authority
Community with Delegated Budget	Governing Body (although any Tribunal award will be enforceable against the governing body)
Community Special	Local Authority
Community Special with Delegated Budget	Governing Body (although any Tribunal award will be enforceable against the governing body)
Voluntary Controlled	Local Authority
Voluntary Controlled with Delegated Budget	Governing Body (Although any Tribunal award will be enforceable against the governing body)
Foundation	Governing Body
Foundation Special	Governing Body
Voluntary Aided	Governing Body

Note also that those Employees who have been employed at a voluntary-aided School since before 1996 will retain the Local Authority, rather than the Governing Body, as their Employer.

Aside from an academic point of interest, why does all this matter? Unfortunately, different regimes apply to different types of School, dependent on the type of School. This is particularly the case in the areas of appointment and dismissal. The overarching framework is laid out in the School Staffing (England Regulations) 2009, the important features of which are detailed below.

Schools Staffing (England) Regulations

The Schools Staffing Regulations govern the powers of the Employer of appointment and dismissal within the maintained sector; broadly speaking delegating authority in appropriate cases for day-to-day matters to the Governing Body in cases where the Local Authority is the Employer. The current version is the 2009 version, and note that there are very similar (although *not* identical) Regulations covering Wales; which fall outside the scope of this work.

There are some overriding duties: for example, the duty to establish procedures for conduct and discipline of staff, as well as the duty to establish capability procedures. The Regulations distinguish between Community, Voluntary Controlled, Community Special and Maintained Nursery Schools (I.e. Those Schools were the local authority is the employer); and Foundation, Voluntary Aided and Foundation Special Schools (I.e. Those schools were the governing body is the employer). For ease, I will refer to these Schools as Types A & B respectively. To give a brief precis of the responsibilities on appointment and dismissal:

Function/Role	**Type A School** **(Community Voluntary Controlled, Community Special, Maintained Nursery Schools)**	**Type B School** **(Foundation, Voluntary Aided and Foundation Special Schools)**
Appointment of general staff	• Governing Body selects, and authority employs under contract of employment	• Governing Body selects and employs • Local Authority may offer advice to the Governing Body
Pre-recruitment checks	• Governing Body responsible	• Governing Body responsible
Appointment of Head and Deputy	• Governing Body must notify the local authority of vacancy.	• Governing Body must notify the local authority of the vacancy.

	• Panel of 3 governors to conduct the selection process. • For Head Teacher roles, Governing Body must notify the local authority of those shortlisted. • Local Authority can make written representations if they think any individual is not suitable for a post. • Local Authority will appoint the person selected. • Process can be circumvented to avoid advertising the role and conducting a selection process where the governing body has a '*good reason*'. • Local Authority can decline to appoint person selected by Governing Body.	• Panel of 3 governors to conduct the selection and appointment process. • Governing Body can refuse to appoint the person recommended by the selection panel. • For Head Teacher roles, Governing Body must notify the local authority of those shortlisted. • Local Authority can make written representations if they think any individual is not suitable for a post. • Process can be circumvented to avoid advertising the role and conducting a selection process where the governing body has a '*good reason*'.
Appointment of other Teachers	• Governing Body must provide Local Authority with a specification for a post for any appointment longer than 4 months. • Governing Body will select – although no statutory selection process (as there is for Headteachers). • Local Authority can decline to appoint person selected by Governing Body.	• Governing Body must provide Local Authority with a specification for a post for any appointment longer than 4 months. • Governing Body responsible for appointment.

Appointment of Support Staff	• Governing Body recommends person it has picked for appointment. • Must provide local authority with identity of person, job specification – including grade and remuneration. • Authority entitled to make representation if it is of the view grade/remuneration is incorrect. • Governing Body must consider those representations and notify the authority in writing of its reasons if they don't follow the recommendation.	• Governing Body responsible.
Appointment of Supply Staff	• Governing Body must ensure pre-employment checks are obtained.	• Governing Body must ensure pre-employment checks are obtained.
School Meals Staff	• Local Authority responsible for appointment, discipline, suspension and dismissal. • Must consult with Governing Body before doing any of these functions.	• Governing Body responsible for.
Suspension of Staff	• Governing Body *or* Head can suspend . • Must immediately inform the Local Authority when a person is suspended. • *Only* Governing Body can end suspension. • Must immediately inform the Local Authority and	• Governing Body *or* Head can suspend. • *Only* Governing Body can end suspension.

	the Head when suspension is ended.	
Dismissal of Staff	• Governing Body to make decision • Governing Body must notify the Local Authority. • Local Authority to terminate the contract within 14 days of receiving notification from the Governing Body.	• Governing Body responsible.

Education (Independent Schools Standards) Regulation 2014

In relation to independent schools and academies, subject to some limited exceptions, staffing issues are covered as far as necessary by the Education (Independent Schools Standards) Regulations 2014. These Regulations provide that pre-employment checks must be conducted before employment (I.e. Appropriate DBS Checks, proof of the right to work in the UK, medical fitness and qualifications as applicable). Similar checks are needed to ensure the suitability of a proprietor of such a School, or the Chair of the Trust where the School is a body corporate - e.g. in the case of an academy/multi-academy trust. Such checks are not normally needed for a member of staff being employed without a break from a maintained school.

Other than the pre-employment provisions, independent schools and academies have a relatively free hand in relation to appointment and dismissal: subject of course to the general law on unfair dismissal, which is discussed later.

Summary

As can be seen, the situation as to the employment status of individuals working within Schools can be quite difficult to ascertain. An audit of the processes adopted within the maintained sector, particularly around suspension and dismissal, is important given the restrictive provisions of the School Staffing (England) Regulations. As ever, the paper trail will be crucial.

CHAPTER TWO
TERMS AND CONDITIONS

Introduction

In this chapter, we will look at the main contractual issues to be aware of in a Schools setting, by reviewing the provisions of the Employment Rights Act; and examining STPCD, the Burgundy Book, and the Green Book. We will conclude with a look at the options and considerations for changing terms and conditions of employment.

The minimum requirement: Section 1 Employment Rights Act 1996

As the law stands, all Employees are entitled to a written statement of the main terms and conditions of employment within 4 weeks of the commencement of employment. It is likely (although not certain) that this right will also be extended to workers; and that the time limit for providing the statement will be reduced. It is, of course, good practice to ensure that prospective Employees are provided with a contract of employment detailing the main terms in advance of the commencement of employment; particularly to ensure that both parties are clear and in agreement with the proposed terms.

The main terms to set out are as follows:

- The name of the Employer and the Employee;
- Date the employment started
- Date when the employee's continuous employment began
- Details of salary/pay (including payment date)
- Hours of work
- Entitlement to Holidays

- Sick Pay provisions
- Details of Pension provisions
- Length of any notice period
- Job title
- Whether the job is permanent or fixed-term – and the date of the expiry of the fixed term if it is fixed term
- Place of work
- Any Collective Agreements affecting the Employment
- Whether or not the Employee is to be required to work outside the United Kingdom

Also note that any change to terms and conditions has to be notified to the Employee in writing within 4 weeks of the change. Whilst most organisations don't miss providing the terms at the outset of the relationship, it is easy to miss notifying the change in writing. Failure to provide either the initial terms or the change to terms can attract a Tribunal award of up to 8 weeks' gross pay.

The Modification Order

The provisions of the Redundancy Payments (Continuity of Employment in Local Government etc.) (Modification) Order 1999, have the effect of preserving continuity of employment at least for redundancy payment purposes within the sector, and more generally between public sector bodies. The Modification Order lists the bodies to which it applies within the Schedules to the Order, and reference to this should be made in the case of any uncertainty. Section 3 to Schedule One deals with Education, and covers all maintained Schools, as well as further education colleges and universities.

Although it is not easy to spot, academies are covered by the Modification Order: specifically at Schedule 1, Section 3: paragraph 8.

The effect of the Modification Order needs to be borne in mind when conducting a redundancy exercise, as this can significantly affect the costs involved; effectively increasing the amount of redundancy payment that might be due. Wherever a redundancy exercise is contemplated, it would be sensible to conduct due diligence of those employees potentially affected, in order to correctly ascertain the position.

The Modification Order does not, however, preserve continuity for unfair dismissal purposes – so although the Employee may be entitled to a redundancy payment, they will not be entitled to claim ordinary unfair dismissal unless they have attained the normal two years' period of service.

The Modification Order also applies to avoid the need to make a redundancy payment where an Employee takes up new employment with another Modification Order body either before before termination, or within 4 weeks. Similarly, the provisions as to 'suitable alternative employment' apply as between Modification Order bodies: entitling an Employee to a statutory 4-week trial period, and entitling an Employer to refuse to make a redundancy payment where an Employee unreasonably refuses suitable alternative employment.

School Teachers Pay and Conditions Document – STPCD

The principal source of terms and conditions for employed teachers remains the statutory School Teachers' Pay and Conditions Document ("STPCD"), which is updated annually (normally in September). As it is statutory, all maintained schools *must* follow its provision; and I would advise anyone managing staff within School to be familiar with its contents, and to refer back to it when appropriate.

STPCD remains relevant for most (if not all) academies, the vast majority choosing to adopt this document as the terms and conditions of employment at least initially on transfer (as of course TUPE prescribes they must do); and thereafter.

STPCD sets out the pay regime for both teachers and senior leaders in Schools; including the requirement for performance related pay, which is dealt with in the chapter on performance management. The document also sets out the contractual framework for teachers at differing levels, including professional responsibilities of both teacher and headteachers; as well as working time requirements: in particular the requirement to be available for work for 1265 hours or a pro-rata equivalent for part-time staff.

Part 4 also contains the provisions regarding allowance for Teaching and Learning Responsibility Payments (TLRs) as well as Special Educational Needs allowances (SEN).

Part 7 sets out the contractual framework and specific professional responsibilities for Headteachers, Deputies, and ordinary teachers, and can be useful to refer to in the event of any disciplinary and/or performance management issues arising.

In the case of a disciplinary or performance related issue, I would recommend phrasing any disciplinary allegation with reference to STPCD. For example, §50.16 could be particularly useful when dealing with an obstructive member of staff, refusing to communicate effectively with the senior leadership team and/or colleagues:

> *"50.16. Collaborate and work with colleagues and other relevant professionals within and beyond the school".*

Although STPCD is not explicit on this point, any term in a contract of employment that contradicts what is said in STPCD is unlikely to be valid. However, do not take the existence of STPCD (or, for that matter the Burgundy and Green Books) as meaning that the Employee does not also need a contract of employment – this should be in place for any employee.

Burgundy Book: Notice Provisions

The Burgundy Book – to give it its full title, the Conditions of Service for School Teachers in England and Wales ,represents the national agreement between the main teaching unions and the local education authorities. It applies to all teaching staff in maintained Schools. In the case of an academy, those Employees who transferred on conversion will be covered by Burgundy Book terms and conditions as they existed at the time of the conversion. Any staff employed post-conversion will not be employed on Burgundy Book terms unless the academy expressly account for this within their contracts of employment. The full document runs to 68 pages; the most current version is as published in August 2000.

The Burgundy Book provides specific notice periods on dismissal or resignation:

> *Teachers resigning their appointments*
>
> *All teachers resigning their appointments will be paid salary;*
>
> *at the end of the Summer term to August 31; or, in the case of a teacher resigning to take up an appointment with another employer to the day preceding the day on which the school under the new employer opens for the Autumn term if this be earlier than September 1;*
>
> *at the end of the Autumn term to December 31;*
>
> *at the end of the Spring term to April 30;*
>
> *or, in the case of a teacher resigning to take up an appointment with another employer, to the day preceding the day on which the school under the new employer opens for the Summer term if this be earlier than May 1.*
>
> *A teacher resigning his/her appointment with effect from the end of the Spring term to take up an appointment with another employer*

should not be required by the former employer to attend the first days of the Summer term if that commences earlier than May 1.

2.2 Teachers resigning their appointments under the terms of paragraphs 2.1 will be required to give notice in accordance with the periods specified in paragraph 4

4. Period of notice and termination of contract

4.1 All teachers shall be under a minimum of two months' notice, and in the Summer term three months', terminating at the end of a school term as defined in paragraph 1 above.

4.2 Notwithstanding paragraph 4.1 above, all head teachers shall be under a minimum of three months' notice and in the Summer term four months, terminating at the end of a school term as defined in paragraph 1 above.

4.3 Notwithstanding paragraph 4.1 above, where a teacher has been continuously employed for more than eight years he/she shall be entitled to receive additional notice, as specified in the Employment Rights Act 1996.

4.4 The provisions of paragraphs 4.1 to 4.3 apply to the termination of a teacher's contract for any reason other than gross misconduct, including dismissal for ill-health and redundancy.

School terms are defined for Burgundy Book purposes as follows:

- *Summer: May 1st to August 31st;*
- *Autumn: September 1st to December 31st:*
- *Spring: January 1st to April 30th.*

The notice periods set out in the Burgundy book create a number of potential issues to be aware of. Firstly, in the case of dismissal for matters falling short of gross misconduct, consideration as to the relevant timing of any notice needs to be considered: both in terms of payment in lieu (and both the STPCD and the Burgundy book are silent on the issue of payment in lieu) and in terms of the service of notice. Secondly, the restrictive nature of the notice provisions can create recruitment problems also; giving Schools little time to recruit, particularly when staff members resign at the end of the Spring term.

Very often, simply the fact of the extensive notice periods can lead to Schools looking to conclude settlement agreements at the end of the Summer term as a means of avoiding, for example, lengthy performance management processes. In those circumstances, it is common for trade unions and/or their representatives to delay the negotiation in order to argue for a later termination date: and concomitantly more money for the member of staff in question.

Burgundy Book: Sickness and Maternity Benefits

The Burgundy book sets out the provisions on sickness and maternity pay applying to teachers. On sick pay, the entitlement is as follows:

During the first year of service	Full pay for 25 working days; after four months service half pay for 50 working days
During the second year of service	Full pay for 50 working days then half pay for 50 working days
During the third year of service	Full pay for 75 working days then half pay for 75 working days
From four years' plus	Full pay for 100 working days and half pay for 100 working days

Note that service for these purposes includes all employment as a teacher with one or more local education authorities. Again, this is a point that should be checked upon appointment. If a Teacher goes from a maintained school to an academy, their entitlement is effectively 'frozen', until such time as they enter into employment in the maintained sector again (unless the academy in question adopts the Burgundy book within their contracts of employment). It is a matter for each individual academy to determine how they will deal with sick leave entitlement, and whether they will honour Burgundy book-style provisions for new starters: TUPE will provide they will have to for any pre-conversion staff. There is a discretion for individual employers to exceed the minimum entitlement for sick leave.

In relation to service-related maternity benefits, the same regime applies. The benefits are as follows:

First four weeks of absence	Full pay, offset against SMP
Next 2 weeks of absence	90% of salary, offset against SMP
Next 12 weeks	Half pay, without deductions unless SMP and half pay would exceed normal amount of full pay
Any further absence	Nil pay up to date of return

To be eligible, the Employee must have completed one year's service as a teacher within a local education authority. Those that do not meet this criterion are entitled to normal statutory maternity benefits. Furthermore, in the event the Employee does not return after maternity leave for at least thirteen weeks, they are to refund an amount determined by the Employer at the Employer's discretion. This does not include any elements relating to statutory maternity pay; and the Employer can also waive the requirement to return for thirteen weeks, or shorten it, again at their discretion. Note also that in calculating the thirteen-week period, periods of school closure are taken into account.

Green Book

The Green Book – to give it the full title, the National Joint Council for Local Government Services National Agreement on Pay and Conditions of Service – applies to all Employees in local government service. For our purposes, all non-teaching staff within a maintained School will be subject to Green Book terms and conditions. In the case of an academy, as with the Burgundy Book, those Employees who transferred on conversion will be covered by Green Book terms and conditions as they existed at the time of the conversion. Any staff employed post-conversion will not be employed on Green Book terms unless the academy expressly account for this within their contracts of employment. The full document runs to 222 pages, and it would be outside the scope of this work to summarise the whole of it.

Green book notice periods (for the Employer) mirror those of s.86 Employment Rights Act 1996 – i.e. One week for each year of service up to a maximum of 12 weeks. An Employee must give a minimum period of notice of the period from one pay period to the next – i.e. For monthly paid staff, one month.

In respect of service-related maternity pay benefits, the provisions mirror those of the Burgundy Book, set out above.

The entitlement to sick pay is as follows:

During the 1st year of service	One months full pay, plus two months half pay once the Employee has completed four month's service
During 2nd year of service	Two months full pay and two months half pay
During 3rd year of service	Four months full pay and four months half pay

During the 4th and 5th year of service	Five months full pay and five months half pay
After 5 years service	Six months full pay and six months half pay

Periods of sick pay can be extended at the discretion of the Employer in exceptional cases. One situation in which this may arise could be in the case of disability-related absences. In any situation where discretion is considered and/or exercised, I would suggest a note is made as to the reasons why the discretion is appropriate to those circumstances; as well as confirming to the affected Employee the reasons for the discretion being exercised and the fact that this is an exception to the norm.

Changing Terms and Conditions

Changing terms and conditions of employment is tricky in any context; yet particularly so in Schools against the backdrop of collective agreements, Burgundy & Green Books and the STPCD. It is not, however, impossible.

Before any change is contemplated a robust business case for doing so ought to be prepared. This is the bedrock of achieving any successful change – since an Employment Tribunal will not normally go behind a well-reasoned business case. This business case will also form the basis of consultation with affected employees.

Once the business case has been established for a change, it is then necessary to examine the actual change proposed. If it is a minor change to terms and conditions, for example, it may be more readily agreed by employees and/or trade unions: and agreement is always the ideal wherever possible. Remember also that a change to long-established working practices could also amount to a change to terms and conditions, even if that change is not written down. For example, the National Education Union (NEU) regard the former 'work to rule' requirements issued under a mandate before that organisation was formed (i.e. when it was the National Union of Teachers) as forming part of their members contracts of employment by reason of custom and practice.

Similarly, it is important to examine any policies and procedures that may be stated to be contractual, as well as looking at the employment contract itself. Furthermore, consideration needs to be given as to whether the existing contract of employment allows for variation, and, if so, under what circumstances and with what period of notice.

Once the contractual nature of the change has been examined, consider also whether any proposed change may be indirectly discriminatory to a particular group; and, if so, whether any mitigation or adaptation of the proposed change is necessary.

Consultation is the next step to undertake: with recognised trade unions and with affected employees. The overriding aim is to reach an agreement. Whilst there is no hard and fast rule as to the length of any period of consultation[1], it should be long enough to enable meaningful consultation to take place. Consider the timing of any meetings – for example, it may not be helpful for any Employees to have a consultation meeting last thing on a Friday afternoon, or immediately before half-term. At this stage, it is important to present the proposed change to Employees and trade unions in order to get their feedback on the proposal. This part of the process will also enable employees and/or trade unions to confirm what impact they perceive the proposal will have; and how important they regard the existing term that you are looking to amend.

Following consultation (which should be at least one meeting, but is likely to be more), if there is an agreement then a change to terms and conditions can be issued to affected Employees. If there is an agreement, the normal notice period for the change can be waived: but in

1 Save where dismissals are contemplated: for more detail, see the Chapter on restructuring

any event it is sensible to phase any change in wherever possible. Notice in this context will be the notice provided for within the contract of employment: and for teaching staff will be in line with the Burgundy book notice periods set out above.

The situation if agreement cannot be reached is more difficult. Any unilateral change to terms and conditions, without agreement, could lead to potential claims for constructive dismissal as well as potential future arguments about the validity of any change. There are essentially 2 options for an Employer in this circumstance.

Firstly, an Employer (particularly where the contract reserves the power to vary the contract) may simply decide to issue affected Employees with a notice to vary the contract of employment, to take effect from the expiry of the notice. The notice to provide in this context is the notice you would have to provide in the case of dismissal. This may be a viable option where the change is not fundamental to the Employment contract and is of a more minor nature, but it should still be approached with caution.

Secondly, and utilised only in situations of last resort, it is possible for the Employer to terminate the contracts of employment of affected staff; and offer to re-engage them immediately on the new terms and conditions. This is, of course, likely to be extremely unpopular, and also carries with it the risk of unfair dismissal claims arising out of the dismissal, as well as the risk that the staff will simply leave for alternative jobs by not accepting the new terms on offer. Whilst the Employer may well have a fair reason for dismissal ('Some Other Substantial Reason', referenced in the chapter on Unfair Dismissal), the fact of the potential claims in and of itself could create a financial liability. Note also that if the Employer embarks on this as a potential option, they will have to complete minimum statutory periods of consultation where more than 20 staff are likely to be affected.

Therefore, whilst it is not impossible to change terms and conditions, any School contemplating this should plan the process carefully, and seek early agreement wherever possible, in order to minimise risk to the organisation. One final note of warning: Employers need to be wary of any change looking like it may be an inducement away from collective bargaining, as this can lead to a potentially significant Tribunal claim, as in the *Kostal* case:

In this case, the Employer was in pay negotiations with Unite. The Employers proposal was rejected on a ballot, leading the Employer to take the step of publishing a notice on notice boards in the workplace, setting out the proposed offer, and the fact that it had been rejected by the Unite ballot. The offer also incorporated a concomitant change to terms and conditions. Crucially, the notice continued by giving individual employees the opportunity to accept the offer individually: with the caveat that if signed agreement was not forthcoming by the 18th December 2015 (9 days after the notice had been posted); the Christmas bonus would not be paid. That communication was also confirmed in writing to the individual employees. The Tribunal and the EAT found this to be an unlawful inducement, and made the award prescribed by statute of £3,800 per employee, per inducement: a liability totalling in excess of £400,000 for Kostal.

Summary

As can be seen, there are a number of important sources of information to consider when looking at the contractual status of staff within School. I would suggest a regular audit of the position, ensuring that up to date documentation is maintained. In addition, any policies and procedures that impact on staffing matters should be regularly reviewed by the Governing Body and/or Board of Trustees as the case may be, particularly if it could be argued that any such policy is potentially contractual.

CHAPTER THREE MISCONDUCT AND DISCIPLINE

Introduction

In this chapter, we will look at some of the issues School should be aware of when dealing with any potential allegation of misconduct, in the context of a disciplinary process. At all times, when dealing with these issues, Schools should have regard to the statutory ACAS Code of Practice on Discipline and Grievance in the workplace. If there is an allegation of misconduct in a safeguarding context, reference should be made to the relevant provisions in *Keeping Children Safe in Education*; as this is the most sensitive area that Schools are likely to deal with, some of the principles to be aware of are set out.

Suspension

The first question that comes to light when dealing with an allegation of misconduct is whether or not a suspension is necessary. It will not be in every case, and certainly ought not to be a knee-jerk reaction. Although historically regarded a neutral act, increasingly Courts are not viewing it in this way. A suspension, will however, normally be necessary to conduct a fair investigation.

In a safeguarding context, Schools and Colleges must have regard to the statutory guidance issued by DfE, entitled '*Keeping Children Safe in Education*'. This document sets out specific rules for staff in dealing with safeguarding issues, and Schools should be aware of, and follow these principles.

When taking a decision to suspend, I would always advocate a written notice being made of the decision, and the factors involved. It is worth noting that the Guidance suggests that suspension should not be the default position and an individual should be suspended only if there is no reasonable alternative. As set out in the opening chapter, the School Staffing (England) Regulations govern who can suspend, and who can lift a suspension in the maintained sector. There are different rules dependent on whether the authority or the governing body is the employer; in both cases the governing body or the head can suspend staff, but only the governing body has the power to lift the suspension. If the authority is the employer, they must be notified of the suspension immediately.

So, what practical advice can be given when determining whether or not to suspend? A non-exhaustive checklist would include the following:

- What is the type of School are you?
- Who has the power to suspend?
- What is the nature of the allegation?
- Does the allegation potentially require a DBS referral?
- Does it require a referral to the Local Authority Designated Officer and/or the police?
- What alternatives are there to suspension?

It would be sensible for the School to make a formal record of their decision-making process, addressing at a minimum the points listed above. Unless there are good reasons for not doing so, it would be sensible to set out the reasoning to the Employee within the correspondence confirming the suspension - this will certainly help to avoid an allegation of breach of mutual trust and confidence; and demonstrate that the suspension was not simply the default position of the School.

It is also worth considering whether the allegation itself could amount to a public interest disclosure; since in that circumstance care must be taken not to subject the 'whistleblower' to a detriment.

A final point to note is that the Education Act 2002 introduced reporting restrictions which prevent the publication of any material that may lead to the identification of a teacher who has been accused by, or on behalf of, a pupil from the same school. Confidentiality in these situations is therefore of the utmost importance; particularly in the age of social media where dissemination of information is both instantaneous and permanent.

I would also make a note – perhaps via an outlook calendar or similar – for the suspension to be reviewed on a regular basis, and to be lifted should the circumstances allow at the earliest possible opportunity.

Investigations Generally

Following a suspension, the next step is to undertake the investigation. The first question will be who to appoint as an investigator. Ideally, it should be someone who has received training on conducting disciplinary investigations; and certainly someone who has sufficient time to conduct the investigation. This is particularly important in cases where a staff member has been suspended on full pay; and in serious safeguarding cases. On this issue, KCSIE gives the following guidance:

> *"In straightforward cases, the investigation should normally be undertaken by a senior member of the school's or college's staff.*
>
> *207. However, in other circumstances, such as lack of appropriate resource within the school or college, or the nature or complexity of the allegation, the allegation will require an independent investigator. Many local authorities already provide for an independent investigation of allegations, often as part of the personnel services that maintained schools and colleges can buy in from the authority. It is important that local authorities ensure that schools and colleges have access to an affordable facility for independent investigation where that is appropriate."* (KCSIE 2019, §206 & 207).

Furthermore, the person investigating the issue ought to be independent; and not a witness to the events that form the subject of the allegations. In many cases, the seriousness of the allegation will inform the choice of the relevant investigator. Any disciplinary investigation has to be 'within the range of reasonable responses'. If there is a risk that the investigation may result in a referral to TRA, for example, School should take the matter far more seriously, than, say an investigation which, if proven, may lead to a sanction of a verbal or written warning.

It is important that an investigator approaches the matter even-handedly, and examines all relevant evidence. Although an investigator does not have to examine every line of argument and/or defence put forward by the Employee, they should if that piece of information or evidence could serve to exonerate the Employee. As ever, Schools should refer to and follow their own policy in disciplinary investigations, as well as the ACAS Code of Practice.

There is no hard and fast rule that says there has to be an investigatory meeting with the Employee prior to referring the matter to a disciplinary hearing; and any investigator should consider this decision carefully. I have certainly seen investigatory meetings produce results that have avoided the need for a disciplinary hearing in its entirety.

There is also a variance in practice as to whether the investigator simply presents a 'neutral' report with no recommendation either way as to whether a case should go to a disciplinary hearing, or whether the investigator makes the recommendation. Either method is fine, provided this is made clear in the policy; and the emphasis is on the disciplinary panel making the decision ultimately rather than the investigator.

There is also a tendency to refer to documents by Appendices. This can produce unnecessary confusion and complexity. I would advocate one file of documents to be produced; in a chronological order and paginated. At the start of the file should be the investigation report, with all relevant documents being listed behind.

Serious Case Reviews, DBS Referrals and Criminal Investigation

In a case involving a safeguarding allegation, Schools (normally the Head, or if the allegation is about the Head, the Chair of Governors) should consult with the Local Authority Designated Officer to agree a course of action. Dependent on the nature of the allegations, and any police investigation, the LADO is likely to convene a serious case review.

I have experience of the notes of a serious case review remaining confidential, and not being disclosed to those charged with investigating a potential disciplinary offence. This of course creates significant problems in both an internal disciplinary and any subsequent proceedings for unfair dismissal. It is important to establish the position with the relevant local authority and ensure that all parties are aware of this in advance of any disciplinary hearing to avoid any unfairness.

However, it is important to remember that the purpose of the serious case review, whilst arising from the employment is focused on entirely different issues to those an Employer is examining. For example, the fact that a serious case review may result in no further action does not mean that no disciplinary rules have been broken, and vice versa. The decision taken by the Local Authority Designated Officer, and for that matter the Police, is only of tangential relevance to a disciplinary situation. What is important is to ensure that all parties know the status of any notes of the serious case review, and get the same disclosure if it is forthcoming; and most importantly that the disciplinary process remains objective and independent of the outcome of either the serious case review or the police investigation.

KCSIE provides that the outcome of any allegation must be recorded in one of the following specific ways:

- Substantiated: there is sufficient evidence to prove the allegation;

- Malicious: there is sufficient evidence to disprove the allegation and there has been a deliberate act to deceive;
- False: there is sufficient evidence to disprove the allegation;
- Unsubstantiated: there is insufficient evidence to either prove or disprove the allegation. The term, therefore, does not imply guilt or innocence.

It is important to note that even in the event of a resignation or agreed severance, there will likely remain a duty on the Employer to make a referral to DBS and potentially the TRA. This can cause barriers to reaching settlements in some circumstances, and I would advocate highlighting the position with the Employee and/or their Trade Union at the outset of any negotiations. The Keeping Children Safe Guidance warns against settlement in safeguarding cases; stating that it will not be appropriate to reach a settlement in the circumstances in which the criteria for a DBS referral are met. The Guidance also confirms that any settlement agreement that purports to prevent an Employer from making a DBS is likely to result in a criminal offence.

Paragraph 163 of the Guidance sets out the criteria for a referral to the DBS:

> *Schools and colleges have a legal duty to refer to the DBS anyone who has harmed, or poses a risk of harm, to a child or vulnerable adult; where the harm test is satisfied in respect of that individual; where the individual has received a caution or conviction for a relevant offence, or if there is reason to believe that the individual has committed a listed relevant offence; and that the individual has been removed from working (paid or unpaid) in regulated activity, or would have been removed had they not left.*

Police investigations will inevitably have an impact on the internal investigatory process. Care must be taken to ensure that the internal investigation does not prejudice any criminal investigation. My practical experience dictates that the Police are aware of the need to conduct an internal investigation; and provided an open line of communication is maintained, and the steps you intend to take are made clear to the Police; they are often content for you to proceed. Of course, the pure time of any police investigation and subsequent criminal process can lead to delays in the process.

It is often suggested that a disciplinary hearing needs to be delayed until after criminal proceedings have been concluded. There is no rule of law to that effect although the matter should certainly be considered with care.

This is particularly important if the Employee in question is in receipt of 'no comment' advice from their criminal lawyer. In those circumstances, those making the decision ought to be advised of exactly the purpose of a 'no comment' interview; and that it does not necessarily imply guilt. It is likely also in that circumstance that the Employee may be advised not to attend any disciplinary hearing for fear of self-incrimination. In that scenario, timing is important. A Tribunal is unlikely to find it reasonable for a disciplinary hearing to proceed shortly before, for example, a final hearing taking place in the criminal proceedings. I would always recommend checking the stage of any criminal proceedings before choosing to proceed with the disciplinary hearing, and making a detailed note as to the reasons why the hearing is going ahead, and the opportunities afforded to the Employee to attend (including the warnings given as to the matter proceeding in their absence in the event of non-attendance).

Children as Witnesses

Inevitably, in a disciplinary situation within a Schools setting, it is likely that the incident may either concern or have been witnessed by children. Gathering the necessary evidence from those children carries with it some challenges. Care should be taken to avoid collusion, and to avoid unnecessary leading: young children in particular may be prone to simply saying what they think is expected of them. When faced with this situation, consideration should be given to the following:

- Production of a method statement detailing the way in which the statement has been gathered;
- The setting of any meeting with the children – to make them as comfortable as possible;
- Taking the statements as soon as reasonably practicable;
- Consideration to inviting the Employee's trade union representative to any such meeting (although again, care needs to be taken not to unsettle the child);
- Making sure the statements are in the child's own words – if they can write them themselves, so much the better;
- Putting the welfare of the child first;
- Informing the child's parents of the need to produce a statement, and potentially inviting them to the meeting – as long as they themselves agree to maintain confidentiality, remembering that Schools have a statutory obligation not to publish information that could lead to the identification of a teacher who is the subject of an allegation by a pupil.

There is no easy way to approach this scenario: it is a difficult one, but following the steps above ought to make the situation as fair as possible. Further difficulties arise where the Employee wishes to challenge the evidence given by children (the ACAS Code gives them the right to); in that case the School must think carefully about properly balancing the needs of the children and the duty of care to the Employee. Whatever decision is reached will of course depend on the circumstances of the case – particularly the seriousness of the allegation – but a clear record of the decision reached, with an explanation of the reason why, ought to made in each case.

Governors as Decision Makers and the Role of HR

Very often in a Schools setting, the decision makers will at some stage be governors. This brings particular problems in advising in this situation; since those making the decision are generally volunteers without in-depth day to day involvement in the School.

Whilst that is good in terms of providing objectivity; without proper training and an understanding of the commitment involved it can be difficult to constitute a panel to hear a case of, for example, dismissal. My practical experience is that it can also lead to delays in the dismissal process whilst a panel is constituted.

In these circumstances, the role of HR advisors can be crucial; although care should be taken to ensure to avoid the errors found in *Ramphal v. Department of Transport*. This was a misconduct case arising out of an investigation in relation to the Claimant's expenses claim and use of hire cars. The HR advisor involved in the investigation, as well as advising on points of law and procedure, also commented on the level of culpability of the Claimant: so much so, that the investigation report went from advising a final written warning, to recommending dismissal. The EAT found the *'lobbying'* from HR to be unfair, and set out the parameters thus:

> *"In my opinion, an Investigating Officer is entitled to call for advice from Human Resources; but Human Resources must be very careful to limit advice essentially to questions of law and procedure and process and to avoid straying into areas of culpability, let alone advising on what was the appropriate sanction as to appropriate findings of fact in relation to culpability insofar as the advice went beyond addressing issues of consistency. It was not for Human Resources to advise whether the finding should be one of simple misconduct or gross misconduct"* (HHJ Serota).

In the *Ramphal* case, the investigating officer was inexperienced; and of course this is likely to be the case when a governor is appointed to conduct an investigation; or for that matter to chair a disciplinary or appeal hearing. It would always be sensible for refresher training to be provided in that situation, simply as part of diligent risk management. Just as the law requires a more careful investigation dependent on the seriousness of the allegation, and its potential consequences logic dictates that the care with which an employer ought to ensure those involved in the disciplinary process ought to be determined by the nature and potential consequences of the allegation.

Remember also that many of the institutions within the Education sector fall within the ambit of the Freedom of Information Act; and in any event experience dictates a greater use of subject access requests pursuant to the Data Protection Act by prospective Claimants: leading to the risk of HR advice being disclosed prior to Tribunal proceedings.

A further point to be certain on is to ensure that the governors in question are as independent as possible in the process. Certainly, care should be taken as a minimum to isolate a section of governors from the issues, to enable them to conduct any potential appeal that may be forthcoming. For that reason, any reports to governors as part of routine gubernatorial business should be careful neither to prejudge the situation nor to refer in unnecessary detail to any ongoing investigation. I would suggest that it is dealt with as a private and confidential item on any meeting agenda.

It is often alleged that governor in question is 'tainted' in some way due to previous involvement with the employee in question. The allegation is essential the same as one of bias. With such an allegation, it is always a question for the individual governor themselves to address. It should not, however, be dismissed out of hand; and I would suggest that any allegation is dealt with within any disciplinary hearing and explicitly recorded both in the hearing minutes and in the outcome letter.

It may be the case, particularly in small School, that sufficiently independent governors are difficult to find: certainly the ones with sufficient spare time. In that case, within the maintained sector, it may be possible to co-opt governors for the hearing from another School within the authority. Similarly, in a multi-academy trust, governors from the local governing body may be available to deal with any hearing. The final resort would be the appointment of an independent person to chair any dismissal or appeal hearing. In any of those scenarios care should be taken from a governance perspective to ensure those chairing the hearing have been given the appropriate delegated authority and/or correctly co-opted to avoid any allegation that any subsequent decision has been made without the requisite authority to do so.

Disciplinary Hearings

As many Schools will have individualised procedures that govern disciplinary hearings, I do not propose to rehearse the detail of an ideal disciplinary hearing. I will, however, give some thoughts on how to proceed.

Firstly, it is important that the proposed timescale and order of proceedings be set out by the chair at the outset of any hearing. This is the time to seek agreement from the parties as to the proposed order, and for them to confirm which (if any) witnesses they will be calling to give evidence. I would also seek clarity at this stage as to whether there are any procedural concerns that a party may wish to raise – and indicate that they should be raised at the outset, rather than during, the hearing. All those present in the room should be introduced; and I would also advocate providing a private area for the Employee and any companion to be able to consult privately, or simply take a break from the process.

It should also be made clear the process for recording the hearing. Minutes are perfectly acceptable, and do not have to verbatim, although if this can be provided it may prove useful. Similarly, the hearing could be recorded: remember though that there is a cost associated with having any electronic recording transcribed. Make clear, however, that if anyone does wish to record the meeting that should be made clear and not done surreptitiously. It is not uncommon for people to try and record hearings through concealed devices: for that reason, it is sensible to ask the parties to take all personal belongings with them when they leave the room.

An example running order for a disciplinary hearing might be:

- Introduction setting out the points listed above
- Presentation of the case by the investigating officer
- Any witnesses the investigating officer wishes to call, and questions to those witnesses by the investigating officer, the Employee and/or their representative, and the panel
- Presentation of Employee's case
- Any witnesses the Employee wishes to call, and questions to those witnesses by the Employee and/or their representative, the investigating officer, and the panel
- Closing statement (if any) from the Investigating Officer
- Closing statement (if any) from the Employee and/or their representative
- Deliberation
- Decision

Ideally, the decision should be confirmed verbally to the Employee within the currency of the hearing, and then communicated in writing. In maintained Schools where the local authority is the Employer, the Local Authority will have to confirm any decision to dismiss in writing to the Employee within 14 days.

Take care in composing the outcome letter. This is probably one of the first pieces of correspondence a Tribunal will read; and it should be sufficiently detailed as to set out the reasoning for the decision in full. It should also confirm the mechanism for any appeal against the decision. Ideally, a finding should be reached against each allegation contained within the letter inviting the Employee to the disciplinary hearing. As well as making findings, the letter should also set out the reasons for the disciplinary sanction applied, and the alternatives the panel have considered before applying that sanction. The test a Tribunal will apply when looking at any outcome on a disciplinary matter is whether the finding is *'within the range of reasonable responses open to a reasonable employer'*. This is a wide ambit, and Tribunals cannot substitute their own view for that of the employer. Clear justification for the decision reached will only assist a School in successfully defending any subsequent claim.

Appeal Hearings

In the main, appeal hearings should follow the same format as a disciplinary hearing. It is important, however, to determine whether the appeal process is simply a review of the decision reached by the disciplinary panel, or whether it is a full rehearing. Reference should be made to the relevant policy on this point.

It is increasingly the case that appeals in a School setting will be conducted as a full rehearing. If that is the case, the appeal panel should focus on all of the evidence presented to and considered by the disciplinary panel. It is not enough simply to focus on the points raised by the Employee in their letter of appeal, which may in any event be quite brief.

If there has been some error of procedure in the disciplinary process or hearing, a fair appeal hearing can remedy that problem: making what would have been an unfair dismissal fair in the eyes of a Tribunal. That is more likely to be the case if there has been a full rehearing of the issues.

As the Employee's time limit for bringing a Tribunal claim runs from the date they were notified of the disciplinary panel's decision, it is important that the appeal is constituted as quickly as possible: this of course will hopefully assist with memories being fresh as well.

Referral to the Regulator

The Teaching Regulation Agency is the regulatory body responsible for investigating allegations of serious misconduct against teachers and headteachers in schools in England. A referral can be made in the case of allegations of serious misconduct against a teacher; and can be made by:

- A teacher's employer (including a supply or employment agency);
- Members of the public
- The Police
- The Disclosure and Barring Service

A referral is only appropriate if the alleged misconduct is so serious that it warrants a decision on whether the teacher should be prevented from teaching. Schools have a statutory duty to refer to TRA in all cases of serious professional misconduct; and must consider a referral whether there is a dismissal for misconduct, or where they would have dismissed but for a resignation by the teacher. Note that as this is a statutory obligation, Schools ought not to derogate from this responsibility, for example when concluding a settlement agreement.

TRA have produced guidance on the factors they will take into account in making decisions leading to the prohibition of teachers from teaching; which Employers should utilise when deciding whether it is necessary to make a referral; if the Employer is in doubt a referral should be made. There are 3 factors that can lead to a referral:

- Unacceptable professional conduct
- Conduct that may bring the profession into disrepute
- Conviction of a relevant offence

The Guidance gives the following examples of what would normally be a relevant offence:

- violence;
- terrorism;
- intolerance and/or hatred on the grounds of race/religion or sexual orientation;
- fraud or serious dishonesty;
- theft from a person or other serious theft;
- possession of class A drugs;
- supplying of illegal substances of any classification;
- sexual activity;
- arson and other major criminal damage;
- serious driving offences, particularly those involving alcohol or drugs;
- serious offences involving alcohol;
- serious offences involving gambling;
- possession of prohibited firearms, knives or other weapons;
- any activity involving viewing, taking, making, possessing, distributing or publishing any indecent photograph or image or pseudo photograph or image of a child, or permitting any such activity, including one off incidents.

If a teacher has displayed behaviours associated with those offences, but have not been convicted, this is nevertheless likely to be unacceptable professional conduct: certainly if the Employee has accepted a caution.

The TRA will normally await the conclusion of any internal process, and a Tribunal process if there is one, before making a decision.

As there is potential for an internal process to ultimately lead to prohibition from the profession, it may in certain circumstances be appropriate for the Employee to be legally represented. In *R (G) v. Governors of X School* the Supreme Court confirmed that the Employee in question ought to be afforded a right to legal representation in the internal process because there was the potential for the Employees Article 6 Human Rights to be infringed: due to the potential for is right to practice in the teaching profession being affected.[1] The facts of the case concerned a teaching assistant accused of sexual misconduct within a primary school.

If a School receives a request for an Employee to be legally represented in these circumstances, the request ought certainly to be considered carefully; clearly the answer will be dependent upon the specific allegations in question.

Summary

As can be seen, dealing with any misconduct issue, but particularly one that may lead to dismissal, is something that should be approached with care. The Employee is likely to be represented by an experienced trade union representative; who certainly within the maintained sector is likely to be experienced in the procedures of the LEA in question. Furthermore, as teaching is at least a profession, and more likely a *vocation* as well, the impact of any dismissal on the Employee is likely to be extremely serious indeed; even more so if it results in a DBS referral and/or a referral to the regulatory body.

Those making the decisions may be inexperienced, and may be volunteers. What they are dealing with could well be vastly outside of their

1 Article 6 confirming *"In the determination of his civil rights and obligations or of any criminal charge against him, everyone is entitled to a fair and public hearing within a reasonable time by an independent and impartial tribunal established by the law"*

previous experience. Furthermore, there is always the temptation – particularly in safeguarding cases – for any potential allegation of harm to a child to lead to blinkered, subjective approach from decision makers, who are, after all volunteering for a role as a governor primarily to further the interests of those children.

CHAPTER FOUR
SAFEGUARDING

Introduction

Safeguarding is, of course, an enormous topic and one that pervades the whole business of running a School. It is not my purpose within this text to go through the whole ambit of safeguarding; but rather to touch on the issues Schools may face in an employment-related context; looking in particular at the need to obtain DBS checks and the Disqualification provisions introduced by the Childcare (Disqualification) Regulations 2009.

DBS Checks

Prior to employing staff, Schools are required to obtain an up to date certificate from the Disclosure and Barring Service; which will disclose criminal offences, and also information about whether the prospective employee is on the 'barred list' if an enhanced check is sought.

The statutory DfE Guidance 'Keeping Children Safe in Education' expects that most employees will need an enhanced check due to the likelihood of them engaging in regulated activity:

> "87. *The level of DBS certificate required, and whether a prohibition check is required, will depend on the role and duties of an applicant to work in a school or college, as outlined in this guidance.*
>
> 88. *For most appointments, an enhanced DBS certificate, which includes barred list information, will be required as the majority of staff will be engaging in regulated activity. In summary, a person will be considered to be engaging in regulated activity if, as a result of their work, they:*

- *will be responsible, on a regular basis in a school or college, for teaching, training instructing, caring for or supervising children; or*
- *will carry out paid, or unsupervised unpaid, work regularly in a school or college where that work provides an opportunity for contact with children; or*
- *engage in intimate or personal care or overnight activity, even if this happens only once."*

I would advocate regular review of your Schools policy on obtaining these checks, particularly if School decides to obtain an enhanced check for individuals that do not automatically fall into the categories listed above.

The Childcare (Disqualification) Regulations 2009

The Childcare (Disqualification) Regulations 2009 go further, preventing Employers from employing those involved in Early and Later Years (in practice under 8-year olds) if that person is convicted of a relevant offence, or if they are on the 'barred list'. The DfE has produced statutory guidance on the Regulations - "Disqualification under the Childcare Act 2006" which applies to local authorities, maintained schools, academies and free schools.

A person will be included on the barred list if one or more of the following apply:

- The individual has been convicted or cautioned for sexual offences against children;
- They have been caution or convicted for other offences (kidnapping, murder, some sexual offences against an adult);
- They are subject to a risk of sexual harm order;

- They are subject to a disqualification order and the DBS has reason to believe they have been or might engage in regulated activity;
- They have engaged in relevant conduct – i.e. conduct which endangers or likely to endanger a child, conduct which would do so if repeated, conduct involving sexual material relating to children or inappropriate sexually explicit images depicting violence against human beings and inappropriate conduct of sexual nature involving a child;
- They satisfy the harm test – i.e. individual may harm a child, cause a child to be harmed, put a child at risk of harm, attempt to harm or incite another to harm a child.

In practice, Schools are unlikely to have employed those individuals; since those matters will have been disclosed upon obtaining the DBS certificate.

Remember that the Regulations only apply to those staff working within and Early Years and/or Foundation Stage settings. This includes both before and after school provisions (e.g. Breakfast clubs and the like). Staff within the following roles are not covered:

- Those who only provide education, childcare or supervised activity during school hours to children above reception age;
- Those who only provide childcare or supervised activities out of school hours for children who are aged 8 or over;

Provided always that those staff also have no involvement in the management of the provision.

Schools are required to make their staff aware of the provisions of the legislation: it is good practice for this to be undertaken as part of regular safeguarding training.

Once a School is aware that a staff member is subject to the restrictions above, the Employer must take steps to ensure that member of staff is no longer employed in the early years provision, our involved in the management of an early years provision without a waiver being received: whether through paid leave or redeployment. Many will inevitably look to dismiss; conceivably the Employer could rely on statutory illegality, but many more will look to some other substantial reason as a reason for dismissal. A more detailed examination of some other substantial reason in an education context can be found in the chapter on Unfair Dismissal.

A member of staff, if they are on the barred list can make an application for a waiver via Ofsted. Schools are required to notify Ofsted upon becoming aware that an individual is disqualified; they must tell the individual that Ofsted has been informed, and the implications of the disqualification.

Summary

Safeguarding is a huge area, and one that pervades almost all aspects of employment law within School. School Leaders and Heads will be better versed than I am in the intricacies, but hopefully some of the information set out in the foregoing chapter will enable more informed decision making throughout the process.

CHAPTER FIVE
RESTRUCTURING

Introduction

In this chapter, we will look at potential issues to be aware of in any restructure/redundancy process; looking at the consultation requirements, and the selection process involved.

What is a redundancy?

Redundancy is defined in the Employment Rights Act in the following way, at section 139:

> *"an employee who is dismissed shall be taken to be dismissed by reason of redundancy if the dismissal is wholly or mainly attributable to—*
>
> *(a) the fact that his employer has ceased or intends to cease—*
>
> *(i) to carry on the business for the purposes of which the employee was employed by him, or*
>
> *(ii) to carry on that business in the place where the employee was so employed, or*
>
> *(b) the fact that the requirements of that business—*
>
> *(i) for employees to carry out work of a particular kind, or*
>
> *(ii) for employees to carry out work of a particular kind in the place where the employee was employed by the employer,*
>
> *have ceased or diminished or are expected to cease or diminish."*

By far the most common scenario in a Schools setting will be the diminution of the need to employ people to carry out work of a particular kind.

It can also be the case that a restructure - that does not necessarily meet the statutory definition of redundancy, can nevertheless result in fair dismissals, constituting a business reorganisation falling short of redundancy.

If an organisation is considering the need to make redundancies, it is essential that they can demonstrate the business need for doing so. A Tribunal will not normally go behind a business case, but they are more likely to make enquiries if the business case is not sufficiently detailed, or substantiated.

It is important to prepare the business case in as much detail as possible before any redundancy process is undertaken. Whilst inevitably costs will form part of that case; I would also advocate that any such business case also sets out how it will meet the aims of the School: for example, by improving learning outcomes.

The important thing to focus on in any redundancy or restructure process is the posts, rather than the people within those posts. If a post is ineffective due to the incapability of the person in that post, then performance management is the route to adopt rather than redundancy.

Consultation Requirements

A key component of any fair dismissal on redundancy grounds is the process of consultation with affected employees. The duty to consult is triggered once a decision is made at board-level to proceed with the redundancy/restructure exercise: in a School setting, this will most often be a decision taken at governing body level.

The law sets out minimum periods of consultation, as follows:

- For 20 to 99 employees, the minimum period of consultation before the dismissals take effect is 30 days;
- For 100 or more employees, the minimum period is 45 days.

Of course, in most Schools cases, none of those minimum periods will apply, since it is normally the case that less than 20 dismissals are contemplated. The duty to consult is with the Employee's representative (i.e. The trade union or other employee representative elected for that purpose); although it is standard industrial practice to consult with the affected employee as well.

The consultation must be about the need to make the redundancies, as well as exploring any means to avoid the redundancy: this can include, for example, job sharing or a voluntary reduction in hours. I would advocate that the business plan is shared with the affected Employees at an early stage, as this will form the basis of the consultation. Consultation should be a 2-way process, so Schools should ensure that they listen and respond to the issues raised by the affected Employees throughout the process.

Given the relative shortness of the School term, as well as the relative length of the Burgundy Book notice periods careful planning of the process needs to be undertaken at the outset. Whilst there is no minimum period of consultation if less than 20 dismissals are contemplated, it should be long enough for a meaningful consultation to take place. It is not enough simply to pay lip service to the process.

An early contemplation will normally be to consider whether to accept applications for voluntary redundancy. Although good industrial practice, there is no legal requirement to do this – although Schools' own policies may include this as a stipulation. Whatever the situation, it should be made clear that School will not be bound to accept an application for voluntary redundancy: this will avoid losing key members of staff, as well as potentially incurring significant pension liabilities, particularly with the Local Government Pension Scheme.

Selection Process

At the same time as consulting with Employees about the redundancy/restructure, consultation should also discuss the proposed method of selection. There are essentially two main options: a selection matrix, or interview.

Prior to proceeding with the selection, however, School will need to decide the 'pool' of job posts which fall to be considered as being at risk of redundancy, and thus in the pool for selection. Sometimes this will be obvious – the School has 4 maths teachers but only needs 3: the pool would therefore be all the maths teachers at School. Sometimes this is not as straightforward, and indeed a pool for selection can be as small as one person. It is for the Employer to justify the basis of the selection pool; but School should be careful to draw the net too narrow in scope, and should have an objective, non-discriminatory reason for their decision.

Once that is done, and following consultation with those affected, a selection method can be employed. A selection matrix involves giving an Employee a 'score', based on a set criteria. Common criteria included with a matrix includes (this list is non-exhaustive):

- Length of service (although this cannot be the only criteria);
- Standard of work;
- Attendance record, being careful not to include disability or maternity-related absences;
- Disciplinary record.

A Tribunal will not normally go behind the scores produced in a selection matrix; however it is sensible to make a contemporaneous record of the scoring and methodology employed. An Employee is not entitled to see their colleagues score, but they should be informed of their score and given an opportunity to challenge it.

An alternative to a selection matrix is to have a competitive interview process. This works particularly well when the School is looking to re-model the roles; for example, to include new responsibilities, or an up-dated job description. Again, notes of the interview process and meth-odology on marking should be made and retained. It is also a good idea to consider providing some interview training in advance; particularly if the affected staff have been employed at School for some time, and therefore unlikely to have much recent experience of interviews.

Redundancy Payments and Suitable Alternatives

Any Employee made redundant with more than 2 years' service in en-titled to a statutory redundancy payment, based on their age, salary and length of service. It is worked out on gross weekly pay, subject to the statutory cap which currently stands at £525 per week. It is also age-re-lated, with Employees being able to claim 0.5 week's pay for each year of service under the age of 22, 1 week's pay for each year of service between 22 – 41, and 1.5 week's pay for each year of service over the age of 41. The maximum number of years than can be claimed for is 20.

The calculation is therefore as follows:

A x B x C

Where:

A = length of service

B = age-related multiplier

C = gross weekly pay capped at £525.

So the calculation for a 50 year old employee, with a salary of £50,000 gross and 20 years service would be:

9 x 1.5 x £525 = £7087.50 (i.e. 9 years over the age of 41)

11 x 1 x £525 = £5775

Total : £7087.50 + £5775 = £12862.50.

However, many Local Authorities and Schools may have more generous redundancy payment schemes in place; for example, they may choose not to have a cap on gross weekly pay.

Throughout any redundancy process, there is a duty on the Employer to look for suitable alternatives to redundancy. This applies even once notice of dismissal has been provided.

An Employer can refuse to pay a redundancy payment if an employee unreasonably refuses an offer of suitable alternative employment. However, an Employer considering this option should tread carefully, as the question of whether a role is 'suitable' is not purely objective one, but will also take the Employee's viewpoints into account. An Employee is entitled to a statutory 4-week trial period in the new role before making a decision as to whether or not they view the role as suitable.

Summary

As can be seen, careful planning is important before embarking upon any restructure process. An agreed procedure can be particularly helpful; and most organisations will always seek to avoid compulsory redundancy whenever possible. I would always advocate making decisions on what is best for School as a whole, and focusing on posts rather than people: although I recognise this is difficult in practice!

CHAPTER SIX
PARENTAL RIGHTS AND FLEXIBLE WORKING

Introduction

In this chapter, we will look at the brief overview of the different types of parental leave, and the rights and responsibilities pertaining to each. We will conclude also with a look at the regime around the right to apply for flexible working, which is now available to all employees. The provisions and entitlements to parental leave are comprehensive and detailed; for brevity I only propose to look at the main issues within this text.

Maternity, Adoption and Shared Parental Leave

Maternity & Adoption leave is split into two periods: ordinary maternity leave (the first 26 weeks) and additional maternity leave (the remaining 26 weeks). The maximum amount of time off is 52 weeks; the minimum is 2 weeks. In practice, this distinction is becoming less important over time, as most employers guarantee that the Employee can come back to the same job regardless of whether they take ordinary or additional maternity leave.

An Employee on maternity, Shared Parental or Adoption leave is entitled to the same benefits as if they were in work. This means that they will accrue holiday whilst on leave: and many employees choose to utilise this at the end of the leave prior to returning to work.

An Employee can have up to 10 Keeping in Touch days ('KIT days') where they can work, and be paid normally, without breaking the period of leave.

Shared Parental Leave is, as the name suggests, simply the sharing of the period of leave between both partners. A maximum of 50 weeks can be shared between the partners; and leave can be taken in up to 3 separate 'blocks'. Whilst the sharing of the leave is still quite rare, it may be that its usage increases over time.

An interesting question has arisen over the provision of enhanced maternity pay: that is, where an Employer contractually agrees to pay more than the statutory minimum: as with the Burgundy book, which provides:

First four weeks of absence	Full pay, offset against SMP
Next 2 weeks of absence	90% of salary, offset against SMP
Next 12 weeks	Half pay, without deductions unless SMP and half pay would exceed normal amount of full pay
Any further absence	Nil pay up to date of return

To be eligible, the Employee must have completed one year's service as a teacher within a local education authority. If they have not, they will be entitled to statutory maternity leave benefits; currently 6 weeks at 90% of full pay, and 33 weeks at Statutory Maternity Pay. The amount of statutory maternity pay is set annually.

If the male partner takes shared parental leave, is he entitled to the enhanced maternity benefits that he would receive if he was a mother on maternity leave? For some time, this issue was unclear: there were two different decisions both saying different things. However, it is now clear (at the time of writing) that it is not discriminatory *not* to pay a father enhanced pay in these circumstances. I think it is important that this point is made clear within the organisations parental leave policy; in order to avoid any potential for conflict.

Paternity Leave

Paternity leave - distinct from Shared Parental Leave – allows employees up to 2 weeks time off following the birth. It must be taken as whole weeks, and must be taken within 56 days of the birth. There is a right to receive statutory paternity pay during the leave, and the employment rights of any employee taking paternity leave are unaffected.

Time off for dependents and parental leave

Any Employee has the right to have time off to deal with an emergency involving a dependant; and School must afford them this time. A dependent in this context is not limited to a child, but rather someone who depends on the Employee for care - this could also include, therefore, a spouse, parent or grandparent. It is distinct from parental leave, which works in a similar way provide unpaid leave to look after their child's welfare.

The time off is unpaid, though it is open to School to agree to pay. It only applies in emergencies, and so wouldn't apply if the Employee knew about the situation in advance.

It is important to have an agreed policy both for parental leave and for time off for dependants. That policy should cover what School expects in terms of notification – including to whom the notification should be made – and detail the arrangements School can put in place regarding pay. It is important in either situation for requests to be dealt with compassionately, and consistently wherever possible.

Flexible working

From June 2014, the right to request flexible working has been extended to all Employees with a minimum of 26 weeks continuous employment. Whilst many organisations will have a specific policy dealing with flexible working requests, the law sets out a fairly straightforward framework in which these requests ought to be made.

Although termed 'flexible working' the actual right is to request a variation to the contract of employment. To qualify, as well as having the requisite period of service, the request must:

- Be made in writing;
- Specify the change requested and when the Employee would like it to take effect from;
- Explain the effect the Employee believes will have on the organisation and how the Employee believes that effect can be dealt with; and
- Confirm whether any pervious application has been made by the Employee and, if so, when.

The Employer must deal with the request reasonably and must also provide a response within 3 months. Although not strictly necessary, it is sensible for the Employer to include a provision for appealing the initial decision: in this circumstance both the original decision and the appeal should be concluded within 3 months of the request unless an extension is agreed in writing between the Employer and the Employee. ACAS have produced Guidance on dealing with such requests in a reasonable manner.

There are, it should be noted, a host of reasons as to why an Employer can refuse to accept a request: and, to be frank, it is difficult to see a situation where an Employer could not 'fit' a refusal in to one of the lawful categories. They are:

- the burden of additional costs;
- an inability to reorganise work amongst existing staff;
- an inability to recruit additional staff;

- a detrimental impact on quality;
- a detrimental impact on performance;
- detrimental effect on ability to meet customer demand;
- insufficient work for the periods the employee proposes to work;
- a planned structural change to the business.

If an Employer refuses for an invalid reason, or refuses to consider the request reasonably, the Employee can make an application to the Tribunal: the remedy is a maximum of 8 weeks' pay.

Clearly, Schools do need to consider such requests carefully, and be mindful that they can come from any Employee: although the majority are still submitted by mothers returning from maternity leave. Even in the event of agreement, a reasoned note ought to be made of the decision. It can particularly problematic, for example, when a number of requests are acquiesced to: there often comes a tipping point at which further requests become untenable which can seem unfair to staff particularly where colleagues have been granted such requests previously. Rather than simply maintaining a paper process, I would advocate at least meeting with the Employee to properly understand the request at the outset; and (particularly if the request is rejected) to fully explain the reasons for acceptance and/or rejection.

Summary

As can be seen, there are extensive rights open to those with parental responsibility; and my experience dictates that the vast majority of Schools navigate these issues with ease: hence the relative brevity of this chapter. It remains to be seen how flexible working and shared parental leave will develop and change methods of working; although as the workforce becomes increasingly agile this is only likely to become more relevant.

CHAPTER SEVEN
PERFORMANCE MANAGEMENT

Introduction

In this chapter, we will look at the subject of performance management with principal reference to the School Teachers Appraisal Regulations; which set out a statutory framework for performance related pay and appraisal. We will then look at particular problems areas in this context, and conclude with a look at sickness and ill-health cases within the sector.

School Teachers' Appraisal Regulations

For teaching staff, performance management by means of appraisal is now underpinned by the statutory framework found in the Education (School Teachers' Appraisal) England Regulations 2012. They apply to all teaching staff in maintained Schools. Although these Regulations as drafted do not apply to Academies; it could be argued that any Academy that adopts STPCD as part of terms and conditions is bound to follow the Regulations, as STPCD requires pay progression to be linked to performance.

The Regulations set out specific requirements for the appraisal of teachers; linking this to pay progression as set out by paragraph 19 STPCD:

> *19. Pay progression linked to performance*
>
> *19.1. The relevant body must consider annually whether or not to increase the salary of teachers who have completed a year of employment since the previous annual pay determination and, if so,*

to what salary within the relevant pay ranges set out in paragraphs 13, 14, 16 and 17.

19.2. The relevant body must decide how pay progression will be determined, subject to the following:

a) the decision whether or not to award pay progression must be related to the teacher's performance, as assessed through the school or authority's appraisal arrangements in accordance with the 2012 Regulations in England or the 2011 Regulations in Wales;

b) a recommendation on pay must be made in writing as part of the teacher's appraisal report, and in making its decision the relevant body must have regard to this recommendation;

c) where a teacher is not subject to either the 2012 or the 2011 Regulations, the relevant body must determine through what process the teacher's performance will be assessed and a pay recommendation made for the purposes of making its decision, except in the case of newly qualified teachers (NQTs), in respect of whom the relevant body must do so by means of the statutory induction process set out in the Education (Induction Arrangements for School Teachers) (England) Regulations 2012(7) or the Education (Induction Arrangements for School Teachers) (Wales) Regulations 2015(8);

d) pay decisions must be clearly attributable to the performance of the teacher in question;

e) continued good performance as defined by an individual school's pay policy should give a classroom or unqualified teacher an expectation of progression to the top of their respective pay range;

f) a decision may be made not to award progression whether or not the teacher is subject to capability proceedings.

19.3. The relevant body must set out clearly in the school's pay policy how pay progression will be determined, in accordance with paragraph 19.2.

The relevant body referred to will either be the Local Authority or the Governing Board, depending on who the Employer is; which is dependent on the type of School.

Judgment of a teacher's standards is to be done by reference to Teachers Standards as set out by DFE from time to time. The current Teachers Standards in relation to teaching are divided between teaching and personal and professional conduct. The teaching standards are as follows (preambled with the phrase *"A Teacher must"*):

- Set high expectations which inspire, motivate and challenge pupils
- Promote good process and outcomes by pupils
- Demonstrate good subject and curriculum knowledge
- Plan and teach well-structured lessons
- Adapt teaching to the strengths and needs of all pupils
- Make accurate and productive use of assessment
- Manage behaviour effectively to ensure a good and safe learning environment
- Fulfil wider professional responsibilities

The personal and professional conduct requirements look principally at behaviours. The overarching principle is for teachers' to "*uphold public trust in the profession and maintain high standards of ethics and behaviour, within and outside school*".

Problem Areas

There are some problem areas to be aware of. Logically, observation of lessons should form at least part of the mechanism for assessing a Teacher's performance; yet teaching unions are opposed to excessive observation; and for the most part insist on no more than 3 observations per academic year, totalling no more than 3 hours.

Apocryphal evidence also suggests that at least one teaching union is opposed to the use of numerical targets as part of the performance management cycle: so the setting of objective targets; and agreement thereon with affected employees and trade unions can be a difficult area. Indeed, when one looks at the Teacher's Standards, pure numerical assessment is self-evidently difficult; as indeed is any accurate assessment against what could be argued are quite subjective standards and goals.

Furthermore, in the case of governors making the decision, it is important that they have an understanding of their responsibilities (perhaps through training) and the role they pay in scrutinising the recommendations presented to them. Simply 'waving through' the recommendations given can create problems in the future; for example, if future performance issues are raised regarding the individual teacher.

Similarly, if there are outstanding grievance investigations this can also hinder the process. I would suggest wherever possible that consideration is given to the appointment of independent appraisers if there are 'live' grievances: although I appreciate this may not always be straightforward. Additionally, long term sickness cases will also present problems, particularly if the sickness is capable of amounting to a disability for Equality Act purposes.

In addition, many policies suggest that the appraisal cycle will not apply if an individual is undergoing performance management: but I would argue it is still important to ensure a pay review process and decision is undertaken.

The timescales involved also present practical problems. My experience dictates that teaching staff – whether at the coal face or part of the SLT – are incredibly time poor. Whilst it is for each governing body to agree their own mechanism of appraisal, it is the accepted norm that the appraisal will have taken place by 31st October; which in practice means before the end of the first half-term. It is evident, therefore, that the temptation to simply fast track the pay decision without careful thought and proper scrutiny could certainly be significant; but this should be avoided for the reasons set out above.

Parental Leave Cases

Clearly, the appraisal of a teacher on long term parental leave may also prove problematic. Although the Equality Act 2010 allows for special treatment to women in connection to pregnancy or childbirth, this should not be afforded without careful thought, as demonstrated in *Eversheds v. De Belin.* In the case, as part of a redundancy exercise, Eversheds applied a selection matrix which, amongst the factors included 'lock up', I.e. The length of time between completion of a piece of work and payment being received. Mr De Belin was in a pool with another solicitor, a female, who was on maternity leave at the time. Due to the maternity leave, her lock up could not be measured, so Eversheds decided to apply the maximum score for the criteria, leading to the redundancy of Mr De Belin. On appeal to the Employment Appeal Tribunal, the EAT held that Mr De Belin had been unfairly discriminated against; since the obligation to afford special treatment to women in these circumstances ought only to be such treatment as is reasonably necessary to compensate them for the disadvantage occasioned by the fact of their maternity leave. In this case, simply awarding the maximum score for lock up went over and above what was necessary.

By analogy, therefore, there is a real risk of discrimination if a School simply decides to award a pay increase for a woman on maternity leave, either by relying on the provisions in the Equality Act specifically, or simply waving the process. Similarly, not awarding a pay increase is itself likely to be an act of discrimination, self-evidently subjecting the woman to unfavourable treatment contrary to the Equality Act. The situation is clearly not straightforward. One view would be to treat the appraisal itself as a keeping in touch day; and to review the information and performance that is in place prior to the maternity leave, perhaps allowing some leeway for the fact that performance might be lower than expected due to the pregnancy. That would certainly go some way to providing special treatment, which must be the right thing to do, but without simply giving *carte blanche*. It is important that whatever solution is adopted, the member of staff in question is informed of the proposed process and how it will apply to her. Careful planning will certainly assist any Employer in this circumstance.

Capability Information

Regulation 8A of the School Staffing (England) Regulations 2009 requires governing bodies to provide information to new School employers (maintained or academies), on request, information as to whether the prospective employee has been the subject of capability procedures. This can be a particularly useful tool on recruitment; particularly where the reference received appears to be the subject of a settlement agreement. Similarly, those drafting settlement agreements within the sector should be careful to ensure that nothing in the agreement derogates from the statutory responsibility this Regulation imposes.

Furthermore, it self-evidently imposes an obligation on the Employer to retain these records: although this should be done carefully, particularly in light of the provisions set out in the forthcoming General Data Protection Regulation.

As a consequence of this provision, care should be taken before embarking on formal capability procedures, not least since this will potentially impact on the Employee's future employability prospects. Salford NHS Foundation Trust v. Roldan, CA [2010] IRLR 721 is authority than an Employer must take more care in an investigation the greater the potential consequences of a dismissal: there seems no logical reason as to why this would not extend to the decision to invoke capability procedures in a Schools context.

Summary

Management of the performance of teachers within the sector is therefore a process that is not as straightforward as it would be for an ordinary employer. There are prescriptive guidelines to follow on appraisal; and care should be taken work with recognised trade unions throughout this process in order to avoid disputes.

Care also needs to be taken in the instigation of formal capability procedures; and absence management will also be a key consideration for those working in and advising the sector. As ever, the School year does not serve to afford significant time for the management of these processes; making forward planning and awareness amongst decision makers of crucial importance.

CHAPTER EIGHT SICKNESS AND ILL-HEALTH

Introduction

Within this chapter, we will look at the management of sickness and ill-health cases in the sector, and conclude with an examination of the ill-health retirement provisions contained in both the Teachers' Pension Scheme and the Local Government Pension Scheme. This is not intended to provide an exhaustive example of an ideal policy or procedure: since all such policies and procedures ought in any event to be tailored to the needs of the individual organisation.

Sickness and Ill-Health Cases

In January 2018, the Liberal Democrats published a response to their mass freedom of information request regarding sickness absence within the teaching profession for the year 2016–17. Focused on England only, the highlights (if that is the correct term) revealed:

- 3,750 teachers are on long term leave for stress and mental health issues (a 5% increase on the year before);
- 1.3. Million days have been taken off by teachers for stress and mental health issues in the last four years;
- 312,000 days were taken off for stress and mental health reasons in 2016/17[1]

Clearly, the sector is one with a high incidence of sickness related absence; not just for stress, although of course that issue garners media

1 https://www.libdems.org.uk/3750-teachers-england-on-long-term-stress-leave

attention. Management of sickness cases within the profession can be difficult, not least due to the regular breaks provided by school holidays.

Whilst the working time rules set out in STPCD are relatively prescriptive, teachers are expected to:

> *"work such reasonable additional hours as may be necessary to enable the effective discharge of the teacher's professional duties, including in particular planning and preparing courses and lessons; and assessing, monitoring, recording and reporting on the learning needs, progress and achievements of assigned pupils."* (STPCD 2017, § 51.7)

Note however, that Governing Bodies and Headteachers have a duty to ensure a satisfactory work/life balance, and to adhere to the Working Time Regulations provisions (STPCD 2017, § 52.4). This is a point reinforced by the NASUWT in their instructions on actions short of strike action, with the following instruction:

> *"Instruction 8: Members are instructed to refuse to implement any existing management-led policies and working practice which have not been workload impact assessed and agreed by the NASUWT"*

Although the Teacher's Pension Scheme does have provision for retirement on ill-health grounds, the bar for attaining this benefit is set high: a teacher must demonstrate that their ability to work as a teacher is impaired by more than 90%, and is likely to be so permanently.

I would advocate that any sickness policy deals with short-term intermittent absences separately from long-term absences. As with any sickness case, thought should be given as to whether a disability for Equality Act purposes underlies the absence; with due consideration to reasonable adjustments.

Paragraph 19.9 of the Equality and Human Right Commission Code of Practice is particularly useful when considering this point:

> *"Where an employer is considering the dismissal of a disabled worked for a reason relating to that worker's capability or conduct, they must consider whether any reasonable adjustments need to be made to the performance management or dismissal process which would help* ***improve the performance*** *of the worker or whether they could* ***transfer the worker to a suitable alternative role"*** (emphasis added).

When considering this guidance, it can be seen that simply extending trigger points, for example, within an absence management policy is unlikely to be a reasonable adjustment, certainly at the point of dismissal. Furthermore, the duty to make adjustments will only arise at the point at which the employee is certified fit to work if the adjustments are made, following *Doran v. Department for Work and Pensions UKEAT 0017/14*.

Note that the duty to consider transferring the worker to a suitable alternative role is likely to extend across the authority where the local authority is the Employer; and dependent on geographical location across the Trust in the case of a multi-academy trust.

In long-term sickness cases more generally, the decision in *BS v. Dundee City Council [2013] CSIH 91* helpfully sets out 3 factors to bear in mind before deciding to dismiss in long-term sickness cases:

> *"First, in a case where an employee has been absent from work for some time owing to sickness, it is essential to consider the question of whether the employer can be expected to wait longer. Secondly, there is a need to consult the employee and taken his views into account. We would emphasise, however, that this is a factor than can operate both for an against dismissal. If there employee states that he is anxious to return to work as soon as he can and hope that he will be able to do so in the near future, that operates in his favour; if, on the other hand he states that we is no better and does not not know, when he can return to work, that is a significant factor operating against him. Thirdly, there is a need to take steps to discover the employee's medical condition and his likely prognosis, but this merely*

> *requires the obtaining of proper medical advice; it does not require the employer to pursue detailed medical examination; all that the employer requires to do is to ensure that the correct question is asked and answered"* (per Dorrian LJ, at §27).

To summarise:

1) How much longer can you as an Employer be expected to wait?

Considerations under this heading may include looking at the likelihood of a return; and it may also be the case that your School may have a 'rule of thumb' as to other situations in which sickness dismissals have taken place.

2) You need to consult with the Employee and take their views into account

Of course, this is normally a point that would arise generally when following the Schools sickness policy.

3) There is a need to ascertain diagnosis and prognosis

I would suggest this is done via an Occupational Health report. Also, at this stage, and prior to any dismissal, consideration of whether ill-health retirement is an option is also necessary.

It would seem sensible to address these points specifically within a dismissal outcome letter where practicable; not least to serve as an *aide memoir* in the event of Tribunal litigation.

Both the Teachers' Pension Scheme and the Local Government Pension Scheme provide generous ill-health retirement benefits provided certain criteria are met.

The Teachers' Pension Scheme is the simpler of the two, requiring that, to be eligible, the ability to work must be impaired by more than 90%, and likely to be so permanently. There is no entitlement if the member is on the 'barred list'; and the entitlement ceases upon the member entering into further employment as a teacher (but not in another role; for example, as a teaching assistant).

The Local Government Pension Scheme Regulations set out an entitlement to one of three-tiers of benefit if the employment is terminated on the grounds of ill-health.

The specific tier a member will receive depends of their condition, its duration and its effect on their ability to undertake gainful employment.

The tiers are as follows:

- Tier 1 – where the individual is unlikely to be capable of undertaking gainful employment before normal pension age;
- Tier 2 – where the individual is not entitled to Tier 1 benefits, and is unlikely to be capable of undertaking gainful employment within three years of leaving employment; but is likely to to be able to undertake gainful employment before reaching normal pension age; and
- Tier 3 – where the individual is likely to be capable of undertaking gainful employment within 3 years of leaving employment (or before normal pension age if earlier) – in which case benefits will subsist until the individual obtains gainful employment.

'Gainful Employment' is defined as paid employment for not less than 30 hours a week in a period of not less than 12 months. Note that individuals in receipt of Tier 3 benefits may request a review by their employer for their entitlement to be reviewed (normally with a view to being placed on Tier 2).

This can of course, create an extra liability for a School faced with such a request if they have to pay a further pension strain (in the case of

LGPS) following an increase in the tier awarded: and the review request may come some time after the termination of employment (up to 3 years). Note also that the Employer has an obligation to review the payment of Tier 3 benefits after 18 months of them being paid: Regulation 37(5). This will involve obtaining a further certificate from an IRMP. The responsibility for this will differ depending on Schools relationship with the relevant local authority and/or the administering authority for the purposes of the Local Government Pension Scheme.

In all cases, it is necessary to obtain a report from an Independent Registered Medical Practitioner (IRMP) before an award is granted. Crucially, the Employer does have a decision-making role, although the Regulations provide little meaningful scope for disagreeing with the view of the IRMP. The authority of the person making the decision is a point to check, with reference to any Scheme of Delegation in place at the establishment in question.

The Department for Communities and Local Government produced in 2011 Guidance on this area, which can be found on the excellent LGPS Regs website, www.lgpsregs.org.

Summary

Management of ill-health and sickness related absence is always one of the most difficult part of any managers' job; and this is particularly so within the education sector. The key is achieving a fair balance between the needs of the organisation and respecting the welfare of the Employee. It is important, however, to follow the policy that it is place, and not to seek to depart from this except in the case of making a reasonable adjustment for a staff member with a disability. Although it may seem like the caring thing to do, departure from an element of a policy (e.g. a particular trigger point) can lead to inconsistency and problems in the future.

CHAPTER NINE
DISCRIMINATION AND THE EQUALITY ACT

Introduction

The Equality Act, introduced in 2010, was an attempt to consolidate into once piece of legislation a hugely significant amount of legislation pertaining to discrimination and equal rights, that had evolved in various forms since the introduction of the Equal Pay Act in 1970; itself followed by the Sex Discrimination Act in 1975, and the Race Relations Act in 1976.

The provisions of the Equality Act – which apply regardless of whether an individual is an employee, worker, volunteer or service user – pervade the whole ambit of School business; and should be borne in mind when making any decision.

The most obvious usage of the Equality Act within an employment context is of course in the context of claims for discrimination. There is no cap on compensation for discrimination claims, and such claims can be brought in the Employment Tribunal regardless of length of service: indeed, it is possible for a job applicant to bring a Tribunal claim if they think they have been discriminated against during the application and/or interview process. There is also no requirement for an Employee or worker to have been dismissed in order to bring a claim: claims can be brought whilst they are still in Employment.

One final point to note at this stage is that it is possible in a discrimination claim for the claim to be brought against both the Employing organisation and the alleged perpetrator of the discrimination themselves: potentially opening up individuals to personal liability. In the event of this situation arising, careful consideration needs to be given to the need to protect the organisation as well as providing proper support (which may include representation) for the Employee in question.

In this chapter, we will look firstly at the definition of protected characteristics; then look at the various forms of discrimination; and conclude with a more detailed look at disability discrimination in the context of reasonable adjustments: which is common area of difficulty for day to day management.

It should be noted that the Equality Act and discrimination law generally is a very complicated, and rapidly evolving, area of law. As such this chapter can do no more than give a general overview of the principles to be aware of; with some practical tips where possible.

Protected Characteristics

The Equality Act defines a set criteria – termed 'protected characteristics' – against which it is unlawful to discriminate. As will be seen, whilst the majority are self-explanatory, some may require a little more thought. They are as follows:

- Sex
- Age
- Race
- Maternity and Pregnancy
- Sexual Orientation
- Disability
- Marriage and Civil Partnership
- Gender Reassignment
- Religion or Belief

It is self-evident that every individual will carry some of these protected characteristics. Note it is not always necessary to demonstrate that a person carries the protected characteristic that is the subject of the unlawful discrimination – for example, if a woman is not promoted because they are perceived to be pregnant (even if, in actual fact, they are not); this may nevertheless amount to unlawful discrimination.

It is also possible (though rare) for discrimination to take place as a result of a person's association with another; if the reason for the less favourable treatment is on the grounds of a protected characteristic. This stems from a case brought before the Equality Act was in force, in which a mother alleged less favourable treatment as a result of her relationship with her disabled son. In brief, her sons condition meant that she was often late and/or absent from work at short notice. Her Employer (a law firm) grew tired of this and dismissed her. Arguing the case all the way to the European Court of Justice, she successfully demonstrated that the reason she had received the less favourable treatment – in this case, the dismissal - was as a result of her son's disability, which was held to be unlawful discrimination contrary to what was then the Disability Discrimination Act.

The point that arises from both of these situations is essentially the same one – it is the *reason* for the treatment complained of, not necessarily the specific characteristics of the complainant in question, that will be the main focus in determining whether unlawful discrimination has taken place.

Philosophical Belief

'Religion or Belief' as a protected characteristic goes further than simply a belief in a recognised religion to encompass a genuinely held philosophical belief. There have been a number of attempts via the courts to accurately define what amounts to a philosophical belief across a number of examples. The best known, and the leading case, is *Grainger plc v. Nicholson*, which concerned Mr Nicholson's genuinely-held philosophical belief in man-made climate change. Although decided before the Equality Act, this case sets out what remains the classic definition as to whether a belief qualifies for protection under this heading; namely that:

1. The belief must be genuinely held;

2. It must be a belief as opposed to an opinion or viewpoint;

3. It must be a belief as to a weighty and substantial aspect of human life and behaviour;

4. It must attain a level of cogency, seriousness, cohesion and importance;

5. It must be worthy of respect in a democratic society, and not be incompatible with human dignity and not conflict with the fundamental rights of others.

In the *Grainger* case, Mr Nicholson's firmly held belief in man-made climate change was capable of amounting to a philosophical belief. It is impossible to describe every such belief that may arise in the workplace; but I would advocate care whenever this issue is raised.

Direct Discrimination

Direct Discrimination is the 'classic' formulation of discrimination, being in its purest form less favourable treatment of another person on the grounds of a particular protected characteristic. So, for example, the woman denied promotion because she is pregnant will be treated less favourably due to her protected characteristic of pregnancy as well as her sex. Similarly, the observant Jewish person sacked for refusing to work on a Saturday (in that relegation, the sabbath day) will be discriminated against on the grounds of his religious belief.

Because the definition involves examining whether treatment is less favourable that the treatment of another person, this necessarily involves identifying what the law defines as a 'comparator'. This can be an actual person: e.g. John and Mary apply for promotion, John gets the job on the grounds that he is male - Mary has clearly been treated less favourably than her comparator, John.

The comparator is not simply limited to actual person(s); but can also involve a *hypothetical* comparator. This is a more difficult exercise, but one which the Tribunal is well versed in; and looks at the situation where it is alleged that a person with the same set of characteristics and circumstances – but *without* the relevant protected characteristic – would have been treated differently.

If proven – the burden is for the Employee to prove facts from which a Tribunal could reasonably conclude that discrimination has taken place – there is no defence to direct discrimination (except in the case of Age Discrimination); unless the Employer can rely on what is referred to as the 'statutory defence'. This defence involves an Employer demonstrating that they had taken all reasonable steps to prevent this discrimination from taking place. In practical terms, that is often very difficult to demonstrate.

As mentioned above, direct discrimination on the grounds of Age can be defended if the Employer can demonstrate that they had a 'proportionate means of achieving a legitimate aim'. Thus, as in the case of *Seldon v. Clarkson Wright & Jakes*, it was not unlawful discrimination for a law firm to have a compulsory retirement age for its partners. The legitimate aims relied on in that case including providing more junior members of staff with an expectation of partnership, facilitating planning of the partnership and the workforce as a whole, and limiting the need to expel partners contributing to a supporting atmosphere within the Firm.

We will return to the idea of a 'proportionate means of achieving a legitimate aim' when looking at the concept of indirect discrimination.

In examining complaints of discrimination, the Tribunal will be focused on the cause, or the *reason why* the treatment complained of occurred. The protected characteristic does not have to be the sole reason for the treatment; but it must at least be a significant influence on the treatment in question.

Indirect Discrimination

Indirect discrimination is where a 'provision, criterion or practice' (PCP) employed by an employer disproportionately affects one group of people with a shared protected characteristic as opposed to other groups.

So, for example, a requirement that all PE teachers be at least 6 feet tall would disproportionately affect women: since statistically more men than women are likely to meet that criteria. It is impossible to list every matter that could be defined as a PCP. Often, it will be employer rules and regulations contained in employment contracts, policies and handbooks – though there is no requirement for it to be written down.

Unlike direct discrimination, for which there is no defence, indirect discrimination can be defended if it can be 'justified'. It is necessary for any employer seeking to justify a potentially discriminatory policy to demonstrate that the policy is a *"proportionate means of achieving a legitimate aim"*.

A number of points flow from this. First, the aim itself must be legitimate. In practical terms, this will often mean linking it to a business or operational need. Simply relying on cost alone will almost certainly not be enough. Whatever the reason for the practice, if an organisation can demonstrate a legitimate aim linked to the needs of the organisation, a Tribunal will rarely go behind legitimate business or organisational reasons.

Take, for example, a sickness/absence management policy: operated by all employers. On the face of it, it could be argued that the existence of that policy – which can, of course, lead to potential dismissal – is indirectly discriminatory to disabled people: the theory being that disabled people, statistically, may be more likely to have time off. However, a stated aim of an absence policy, for example, to reduce workplace absence, ensure the smooth operation of the organisation, preserve costs and assist the wellbeing of staff is likely to be a legitimate aim. Taking that one step further, a School particularly ought to be able to demonstrate this with reference to their absence policy: firstly, the costs incurred in securing supply staff *and* (remembering that cost alone is unlikely to be enough) the potential impact on learning outcomes for pupils taken together should be a legitimate aim.

A legitimate aim alone is not enough: any PCP must be proportionate to the issue it is intended to address as well as the way in which it is introduced. Utilising the absence example above, a sudden change to policy leading to a potential dismissal hearing after 3 absences could well fall foul of proportionality.

My advice would be to review any existing practices within School and satisfy yourself that the reasons for them are both written down (I would suggest as an opening paragraph to the policy), and linked to the overall business aims of the School. This also ought to be part of the consideration taken into account both on the introduction of any new policy as well as during any process of recurring review.

Harassment

Harassment is an increasing topic of importance, following the #metoo movement and the Weinstein allegations. The increasing use of social media also unfortunately leads to further potential routes in which individuals could be harassed.

Within this section we will deal with harassment in the sense it is defined in the Equality Act. We will not touch on the provisions of the Protection from Harassment Act 1997, which fall outside the scope of this work.

Harassment is set out in the Equality Act as:

> *"Unwanted conduct related to a relevant protected characteristic that has the purpose or effect of*
>
> > *(i) violating [a person's] dignity;*

> *(ii) creating an intimidating, hostile, degrading, humiliating or offensive environment [for them]"*

As with a direct discrimination claim, both the alleged harasser and the organisation can be liable. Whilst it perhaps most commonly cited in relation to unwanted sexual conduct of a sexual nature, harassment can be on the grounds of any protected characteristic.

The law takes into account both the actual effect on the victim, as well as whether objectively the treatment could be said to have the requisite effect. An example of how this works out in practice was a case brought by an employee who worked in the newsroom of a national newspaper. The Claimant in that case had strong held religious belief, and brought a claim for harassment on the basis that they had been subject to an intimidating, hostile, degrading, humiliation or offensive environment. The treatment complained of was overhearing a colleague exclaiming *"What's happened to the fu—ing Pope"* following the resignation of Pope Bendedict XVI. Whilst the Tribunal did not doubt the evidence of the Claimant, the claim failed on the basis both that the comment was not directed to the Claimant, but also that it would not be reasonable to expect – within the context of busy newsroom in which 'industrial' language was not uncommon – that the comment would create the environment complained of.

Clearly, any allegation of harassment in the workplace should be taken very seriously indeed, and investigated in line with the organisations stated policy. A defence is available if an Employer can demonstrate that they have taken all reasonable steps to prevent the harassment from taking place. Whilst this is in practice difficult to demonstrate, regular training on Equality & Diversity issues can assist. What is equally important is ensuring that the workplace culture hits the right note, and that care is taken to understand the individual needs amongst the workplace. Managers in particular have a key role in setting the standard and ensuring that what may be perceived simply as friendly banter does not cross the line into becoming offensive.

It is also a sensible idea to have a relationships at work policy amongst staff members to set out the standard required.

Victimisation

Like harassment, victimisation in an Equality Act sense is different from that understood in common parlance. Originally designed to ensure that discrimination claims could be brought, by providing statutory protection for those assisting people bringing victimisation claims, victimisation is defined as follows in the Equality Act (s.27):

> "*Victimisation*
>
> *(1) A person (A) victimises another person (B) if A subjects B to a detriment because—*
>
> *(a) B does a protected act, or*
>
> *(b) A believes that B has done, or may do, a protected act.*
>
> *(2) Each of the following is a protected act—*
>
> *(a) bringing proceedings under this Act;*
>
> *(b) giving evidence or information in connection with proceedings under this Act;*
>
> *(c) doing any other thing for the purposes of or in connection with this Act;*
>
> *(d) making an allegation (whether or not express) that A or another person has contravened this Act.*
>
> *(3) Giving false evidence or information, or making a false allegation, is not a protected act if the evidence or information is given, or the allegation is made, in bad faith.*"

As can be seen, the definition of 'protected act' goes further than just assisting another person in bringing an Equality Act complaint (for example, by providing a witness statement in a Tribunal case); but covers 'any other thing' done for, or in connection with, Equality Act purposes. This could include, for example, the raising of a grievance (potentially even an informal grievance) about potentially unfair treatment.

It is also important to bear in mind that detriment goes further than less favourable treatment. It is normally defined as treatment that the ordinary person might regard as 'unfavourable'. In a harassment complaint, for example, a common response is to remove the purported victim from the department in which the perpetrator operates "for their own protection". This is certainly something that could amount to a detriment, and could therefore leave an organisation open to a claim of victimisation in that circumstance.

Care should therefore be taken whenever a grievance (both informal and formal) is intimated, to examine whether it could potentially constitute a complaint concerning Equality Act issues. If it does, then care should be taken not to subject the complainant to anything that could be regarded unfavourable.

Disability and Reasonable Adjustments

Within this section we will focus both on the definition of disability in a legal sense, and the duty that imposes upon Schools to make reasonable adjustments on account of the disabilities of staff members. Note that of course the duty to make reasonable adjustments goes further that just accommodating the needs of staff members, and includes both learners and service users - although that is beyond the scope of this work.

Disability – definition

The Equality Act defines disability in this way (s.6):

Disability

(1) A person (P) has a disability if—

(a) P has a physical or mental impairment, and

(b) the impairment has a substantial and long-term adverse effect on P's ability to carry out normal day-to-day activities.

Whether a person has a disability is a legal decision for the Courts, and not a medical one: though of course information from medical practitioners will be invaluable in the making of a determination. It is for this reason that some Occupational Health experts will refuse to give a definitive view on the question of disability.

Some medical conditions automatically meet the definition of disability from the point of diagnosis, without any further examination. They are:

- Cancer
- HIV
- Multiple Sclerosis

Any other physical or mental impairment will be assessed with regard to the criteria set out above. In this context, 'long-term' is regarded as either lasting, or likely to last, for 12 months or more.

Day to day activities is also defined broadly: and Schools should be wary of assuming that simply because a staff member is functioning without impairment at work that their condition will not have adverse effects on their day-to-day activities. The effect of working through the day may render them so tired that they are unable to continue normal day-to-day activities at the end of the working day.

In any case where an individual may potentially have a disability, it would be wise to seek advice from an Occupational Health adviser. Whilst it may be tempting to seek a report from the staff members own GP, I would advocate against this. The function of the GP is to determine and treat illness: the function of an OH adviser is to determine whether they staff member can return to work (and if not, when they are likely to be able to); and to suggest any reasonable adjustments.

Disability – knowledge

For any employee to be successful in a claim of disability discrimination, it is necessary for them to demonstrate that the employer knew they had a disability; or that the Employer *ought to have known*. In many circumstances, this will be clear cut, as either the Employee has declared their impairment, or it has been confirmed through an OH report.

An Employer is not entitled to stick their head in the sand – if a Tribunal concludes that a reasonable employer would have become aware of the Employee's disability, that Employer will be treated as though they were aware of the disability: even if in actual fact they were not aware. In this context, a Tribunal may, for example, examine whether the Employer has followed its own policies in order to assess whether the Employer ought to have known of the disability. So, if an Employer has routinely failed to conduct return to work interviews following periods of absence, a Tribunal could conclude that if the Employer had followed that element of their policy, they would have become aware of the disability.

Reasonable adjustments

A staff member who has a disability is entitled to 'reasonable adjustments'. Whilst some reasonable adjustments may be obvious – e.g. the installation of a ramp or lift to overcame stairs – this will note always be the case; and it is impossible to create a definite list of what will, and will not be, a reasonable adjustment.

A failure to make a reasonable adjustment can result in a successful claim to the Employment Tribunal (though this claim is often brought as an adjunct to wider claims of discrimination).

The requirement to make a reasonable adjustment is triggered if the employer has in place a provision, criterion or practice ('PCP') which places a disabled person at a substantial disadvantage compared to non-disabled people.

The operative phrase here is 'substantial'; though in practice many employers are happy to (and should) accommodate small adjustments even in situations where the disadvantage suffered is not substantial.

Being pro-active in this area can assist greatly; discussing with the staff member what adjustments will assist; as well as conducting risk assessments as to the working environment. If the organisation is in a position where they need to refuse a request for a reasonable adjustment, it is important to make a careful note of why the adjustment has been refused, and the grounds for doing so: i.e. the adjustment is not reasonable; or the disabled person is not placed at a substantial disadvantage.

What is reasonable in the circumstances will depend on a number of different factors, including the size and resources of the employer. If cost is an issue, it is important to be clear as to the actual budgeting process, and the steps the employer has taken to investigate the proposed adjustment. An employer that says to a Tribunal *"Well, it just wasn't reasonable"*, without any documentary evidence, is unlikely to be persuasive.

If the question is whether the disadvantage is substantial, any employer should tread very carefully indeed. At the very least, I would advocate a OH report into the disability and the limitations that this places on the employee in order to make an informed decision as to whether the organisation's particular PCP places disabled people at a particular disadvantage.

Discrimination 'arising from a disability'

Section 15 of the Equality Act provides further protection for disabled people, providing them with the ability to bring a claim if a person treats them 'unfavourably' because of something arising in consequence of a disability.

So, for example, a dismissal as a result of disability-related absence is likely to be unfavourable treatment arising from that staff members disability. However, this strand of discrimination can be defended if an organisation can demonstrate that the action taken amount to a proportionate means of achieving a legitimate aim: which is discussed in further detail in the section on indirect discrimination. In any claim for failure to make reasonable adjustments, an employee is likely to claim under this section as well.

A different example of a successful claim in this context came in the case of *Land Registry v. Hoghton*. In that case, the Employer operated a provision that any employee under a written warning for absence would not be entitled to share in the bonus provision they operated. The Claimants in that case were all under written warnings for disability-related absences. The tribunal agreed that this amount to unfavourable treatment arising in consequence of their disability; and rejected the Employers argument that they had a proportionate means of achieving a legitimate aim.

Unlike direct discrimination, it is not necessary in a claim of this nature to identify a comparator: the Courts will simply look at whether there has been unfavourable treatment, and if so, whether that treatment arises from a disability.

The section on sickness and ill-health deals with reasonable adjustments in a sickness context in more detail.

Compensation & Injury to Feelings

Whilst claims for unlawful discrimination can be brought in both the Courts and the Employment Tribunal, by far the most common route is via the Employment Tribunal.

If successful, a Tribunal can make a declaration that a person has been unlawfully discriminated. That person is also entitled to receive compensation. The compensation will be all loss flowing from the discrimination; and can include, for example, loss of earnings. In the most serious cases, this could include entire career loss: there is no cap on compensation for discrimination claims, and the current highest award made by a Tribunal is £4.5 million: although this is the exception rather than the rule.

It is possible, in a discrimination case, to make a claim for injury to feelings. If successful, a Tribunal will make an award based on the *Vento* guidelines, which classifies awards for injury to feelings into three bands:

1. The lower band: For one-off or less serious acts of discrimination – £900 to £8,800

2. The middle band: £8,800 to £26,300

3. The upper band: the most serious acts of discrimination: £26,300 to £44,000 (although really serious cases can go above this).

Summary

Discrimination in the workplace is a massive topic in and of itself. This chapter cannot give a comprehensive overview of what is an incredibly complicated area of the law, but hopefully gives School Business Leaders and Headteachers an insight into the areas to be aware of: as well as a trigger for when further advice might be needed.

CHAPTER TEN
TUPE

Introduction

In this Chapter we will look at the practical implications of the Transfer of Undertakings (Protection of Employment) Regulations (TUPE for short) for Schools; highlighting the following:

- The situations in which a transfer can occur
- The effect of a transfer on the Employees
- The need for consultation – what to do, when to do it, and what to say
- What your obligations are in terms of providing information in a transfer situation
- The provisions allowing for changes to contracts of employment post-transfer

Before looking at those provisions, I would make the following points:

1. A TUPE transfer happens by operation of law. It is a little like being able to vote (or legally buy a drink) when you are 18: it happens whether you like it or not, it is not a matter of choice.
2. A TUPE situation is nothing to be concerned about as an employer: providing the process is planned and managed, it can happen smoothly and without exposing the School to risk.

Relevant Transfer

There are 2 situations in which what the Regulations call a *"relevant transfer"* will occur:

1. A Transfer of Undertakings;

2. A Service Provision Change.

Whilst there has been a lot of litigation about what is and is not a relevant transfer, in the vast majority of situations, the position will be clear.

Transfer of Undertakings

This is the most straightforward situation to describe: broadly speaking it covers the sale and purchase of a business, for example; or a change in ownership of an organisation (provided that is not simply a share sale) - any situation in which the assets of an organisation is transferred. In a School setting, the most common situation in which this type of transfer will occur is on academisation, whether into a multi-academy trust or conversion from a maintained school into a stand-alone academy. The more difficult area to consider is in the realm of service provision change.

Service Provision Change

A Service Provision Change (referred to as a 'SPC' for short) will occur when a person or an organisation providing services to another ceases to provide those services, and those services are instead provided by another person/organisation. It will occur when those services are taken in-house. For example, your School may sub-contract cleaning services to a private cleaning company, rather than employing the staff yourself. If you become dissatisfied with that provider, and decide to change, that is likely to constitute an SPC - with the perhaps unintended consequence that you will retain the same cleaning staff with whom you were dissatisfied! Similarly, you may decide to take the service in-house by employing the cleaning staff directly: again, that is a service provision change.

It does not take effect if the services being provided are for a single specific event or task of a short-term duration; or if the services provided are purely the supply of goods or services

Organised Group of Employees

In an SPC scenario, there must be an 'organised grouping of employees' for the transfer to take effect: these are the employees that will transfer. Identifying whether an organised group is in place can be difficult in practice. Following substantial case law, the Courts will now look at the following four steps:

1. Identifying the service being provided;
2. Listing the activities which the staff of the service provider performed to provide the service;
3. Identifying the employee or employees of the service provider who ordinarily carried on those activities;
4. Considering whether the service provider organised the employees into a 'grouping' for the principal purpose of carrying out the activities.

So, in the context of a change of cleaning provider, for example, the steps would be as follows:

1. Identifying the service being provided; – *Cleaning*
2. Listing the activities which the staff of the service provider performed to provide the service; – *Cleaning school premises*
3. Identifying the employee or employees of the service provider who ordinarily carried on those activities; – *Names of cleaners*

4. Considering whether the service provider organised the employees into a 'grouping' for the principal purpose of carrying out the activities. – *Is it always the same cleaner?*

Point (4) is the crucial one. If the cleaners change from day to day, there may not be an SPC as there may not be an organised grouping of employees. However, in practice of course, that would be a fairly unusual setting.

Effect of a relevant transfer

The effect of the transfer is that the Employees will transfer to the new Employer with their existing terms and conditions intact. Any liabilities pertaining to the Employees will also transfer: so it is important, wherever possible, to seek appropriate indemnities from the previous Employer against any wrong-doing or unfair treatment that may have occurred. Any change to terms and conditions will be void, unless it can be demonstrated to be for an *"economic, technical or organisational"* reason: on which more later.

TUPE Consultation

The TUPE provisions require that all those employees who will be affected by the transfer be consulted before the transfer happens. Note, therefore, the need to consult not only with those employees transferring out (or in, as the case may be) but also with those employees who will be affected by the transfer even though they themselves might not be the subject of the transfer. For example, in a multi-academy trust that gains a large School, it may be necessary to consult with, say, existing School Business Managers if there is to be a change to working methods following the taking on of the new School.

The consultation must take place long enough before the transfer as to enable 'meaningful' consultation. In practice, I would suggest that consultation should begin as early as possible, and certainly once a decision has been taken on a formal basis to the events that necessitate the transfer.

Consultation will normally take place with trade union representatives, and/or any employees elected for the purpose. In the unlikely situation where there are no representatives already in place at School, the TUPE Regulations set out requirements for electing representatives. Wherever possible, I would also advocate consultation with the affected employees themselves – obviously giving them the right to be accompanied at any meeting.

Any consultation must cover:

- The fact of the transfer, the reasons for it, and the timescale;
- Any social, legal or economic implication for the affected employees – this could include, for example, a change in location of the workplace
- Any measures that may affect the Employee
- Details of any agency workers employed

Any TUPE situation can be stressful, particularly for outgoing employees so it is important to handle the situation sensitively.

If an Employer fails to consult properly on a TUPE transfer, they face a potential liability of up to 13 weeks gross pay per affected employee.

Employee Liability Information

The TUPE Regulations provide that employee liability information (sometimes referred to by the acronym 'ELI') be provided in advance of any transfer. The information that should be provided is as follows:

- Identity (usually the name) and age of the employees who will transfer.
- Information contained in their 'statements of employment particulars', such as written statement of pay, hours of work, holidays and so on (usually contained in the employee's offer letter or contract of employment).
- Information about any relevant collective agreements.
- Details of any disciplinary action taken against an

  employee in the last two years.
- Details of any grievance action raised by an employee in the last two years.
- Details of any legal action (before the court or employment tribunal) brought against the employer by an employee in the last two years and information about any potential legal action.

The information must be provided at least 28 days prior to any transfer; and a failure to provide does give rise to a potential claim in the Employment Tribunal. Disclosure of this information, will not fall foul of your GDPR/Data Protection obligations since it is a statutory obligation. It is open to the party receiving the staff to request further information also: although of course the transferor will not be obliged to provide this information. One thing to consider requesting is details of how long individual employees have been assigned to the contract/grouping of resources in question; since it is not unknown for unscrupulous employers to use a TUPE transfer as a convenient means of disposing of problematic employees.

One other point to check, if it is not provided automatically in the statement of employment particulars, is ant agreed patters of working; as well as details of any flexible working requests that have been submitted and/or agreed to.

Changes following a TUPE transfer

Any change to terms and conditions following a TUPE transfer for a reason contacted to the transfer will be void, unless the organisation can demonstrate an *'economic, technical or organsiational'* for the change. It is also necessary to demonstrate that ay TUPE-related change entails also a change to the workforce. So, to summarise, there are 2 ways in which a change to terms and conditions can be affected post-transfer:

1. If the change is untreated to the transfer; *or*

2. If the change is for an economic, technical or organisational reason entailing changes to the workforce.

Beneficial changes to terms and conditions will not normally present an issue. Whatever the situation, if changes are planned it would be sensible to consult about these in advance of the transfer. It is also important to document the rationale for any change - particularly if you are to rely on the argument that the change is unconnected to the transfer. It is difficult to give an exhaustive list of reasons that would be unconnected to the transfer.

Whatever the situation, proper consultation with all affected staff - not necessarily just those transferring – as well as with recognised trade unions is vital to avoid the risk of legal challenge.

More detail on changing terms and conditions generally is provided in the chapter relating to terms and conditions above.

Summary

Much like a restructure, a proposed TUPE transfer takes careful planning; and comprehensive consultation with affected employees. Many organisations will try to use comprehensive and complicated methods to avoid TUPE: in many situations this does not work. Far better to accept the fact of the TUPE transfer, to plan for it, and to work with employees and trade unions to achieve the best possible outcome for all affected employees.

CHAPTER ELEVEN
TRADE UNIONS AND INDUSTRIAL RELATIONS

Introduction

Education is the most unionised sector in the country; with 48% of staff being members of recognised trade unions. We have already seen the effect Trade Unions can have on the efficacy of management within educational establishments. It is certainly my experience that trade unions in this sector are amongst the most active; and, at times, militant. In this chapter we will look at the following:

- The changes brought in by the Trade Union Act 2016
- Industrial relations generally
- Facility Time
- Action short of strike action
- Strike Action
- Disciplinary Action and Trade Union representatives
- The Right to be Accompanied

Trade Union Act 2016

The Trade Union Act 2016 dramatically changes the landscape for any trade unions. In force on the 1st March 2017; some key changes to be aware of are:

- Ballot thresholds are now increased to a 50% turnout;

- The ballot paper must set out the nature of the issues, the type of action called for and the time period for such action;
- The voting paper must include a more detailed description of the dispute and the proposed action;
- Unions are required to give 2 weeks' notice of industrial action (although both parties can by agreement lower this to 7 days);
- The mandate will be taken to have expired within 6 months of the date of the ballot; or no longer than 9 months where agreed by the union and the employer;
- Unions must appoint a picketing supervisor;
- The power to introduce Regulations to control the cost of facility time within the public sector: we have seen the first of these with The Trade Union (Facility Time Publication Requirements) Regulations 2017.

It is too early at this stage to accurately assess the impact of the Act; but undoubtedly it will make formal industrial action harder to get off the ground. My team has seen a marked increase in union activity recently: whether this is just coincidence or a move to appear more relevant in the eyes of trade union member is a point of debate.

Facility Time

Facility time is the time afforded by an Employer to trade union officials for them to carry out their trade-union related activities. It is often regulated by a collective agreement; this may be between the LEA and the Union, so any academy that does not have a copy of any such agreement would be wise to seek a copy of this from the LEA. As it is unlawful to subject any person to a 'detriment' as a result of undertaking any trade union activities (wider than just exercising the right to facility time), care needs to be given to understanding the remit of any facility time agreement.

The Trade Union (Facility Time Publication Requirements) Regulations 2017, which came into force on the 1st of April 2017, require maintained schools and academies with more than 49 full-time equivalent employees to publish on their website relating to facility time, by answering the following questions:

1. What was the total number of your employees who were relevant union officials during the relevant period?
2. How many of your employees who were relevant union officials employed during the relevant period spent a) 0%, b) 1% - 50%, c) 51%-99% or d) 100% of their working hours on facility time?
3. Provide the percentage of your total pay bills spent on paying employees who were relevant union officials for facility time during the relevant period;
4. As a percentage of total paid facility time hours, how many hours were spent by employees who were relevant union officials during the relevant period on paid trade union activities?

The relevant period is 12 months from the 1st April, and began on the 1st April 2017: publication must have been done before the 31st July 2017.

Documentation of the actual facility time agreement can on occasion be problematic and a source of dispute: particularly where the agreement is long-standing. Any arrangement should certainly from part of due diligence prior to an academy conversion.

The DfE has produced guidance on the managing of facility time in maintained schools and academies. This non-statutory guidance provides parameters as to what DFE regards as a 'reasonable' amount of time off for trade union activities; and confirmed their view that no teacher funded by the taxpayer should work full time on union work.

DFE also expects all trade union representatives to spend the majority of their working hours carrying out their school-based jobs.

The Guidance also recommends consideration of the following points when receiving a request for facility time:

- *"Can the school accommodate the amount of time requested, and ensure adequate cover for safety and the provision of educational services?*
- *Does the request contain the right information (e.g. purpose, time and place - including agendas of meetings where appropriate), and has enough advance notice been given to provide alternative cover arrangements where necessary?*
- *Does it attract paid or unpaid time (i.e. will the time be used to undertake specific trade union duties, or for activities which should not attract paid time off)?*
- *If the request cannot be accommodated is there a reasonable alternative?"*

Obviously, further thought may be given by the School given the publication requirements as well. As standard, wherever a request is refused or accepted, either the reasons why or (as the case may be) the specific arrangements agreed to ought to be recorded in writing.

Action Short of Strike Action

The NASUWT are currently asking their members to participate in action short of strike action. Formerly, the NUT – now the National Education Union – was also instructing its members to participate in this action. The NEU has not held a ballot on action short of strike action since its formation, so those teachers ought not to still be participating in the action; although the NEU does regard the changes made as part of action short of strike action to be permanent changes[1] to working practices.

Those advising Schools with NASUWT cohorts should familiarise themselves with the relevant instruction/guidance. Both are stated to apply to academies as well as maintained schools, regardless of whether the academy in question has adopted STPCD.

By way of example, returning back to the theme of appraisal, the NASUWT's guidance can be restrictive:

> *"Instruction 1: Members are instructed not to participate in any appraisal/performance management process which does not conform to all elements of the NASUWT appraisal/performance management checklist and the classroom observation protocol.*
>
> *Instruction 2: Members are instructed not to participate in any form of management-led classroom observation in any school which refuses to operate a policy of a limit of a total of three observations for all purposes within a total time of up to three hours per year."*

Strike Action

In the event of a successful ballot for strike action, an early consideration will be the potential for injunctive relief to prevent that action. Whilst of course possible in the relevant circumstances, further negotiation is always preferable to try and resolve the dispute. I would always advocate attempting to utilise the services of ACAS if appropriate; not least due to the potential for adverse publicity as well as the obvious detrimental impact upon pupils at the School.

Should a strike prove inevitable, it is important to control the situation. Although the union are now required to provide a picket supervisor,

1 https://neu.org.uk/sites/neu.org.uk/files/NEU201_Tackling_workload_together_2017.pdf

nevertheless I would advocate clear instructions to staff about their right not to be deterred from crossing a picket line; together with appropriate arrangements for staff who feel unable to cross the line. Worthy of note also is to ensure the correct deduction of pay for strike action (1/365), as confirmed by the Supreme Court in *Hartley and oths v. King Edward VI College*. Strike days do not count as pensionable service for either the Teacher's Pension or the Local Government Pensions Schemes.

The DfE have produced non-statutory guidance on handling strike action in Schools. This makes it clear that the Headteacher must take steps to ensure that the School must remain open for as many schools as reasonably possible. The decision on whether to open the School will be one for the Headteacher; save in Academy trusts where the decision falls to the trust, albeit that in most cases the decision-making power will be delegated to the Head. Headteachers, in line with the guidance, are entitled to ask staff member whether intend to strike; although staff could choose note to answer that question. Whilst a Head may ask other teachers to cover for strike action, staff cannot be compelled to provide cover: §52.7 STPCD: *"Teachers should be required to provide cover in accordance with paragraph 50.7 only rarely, and only in circumstances that are not foreseeable"* – by the very nature of the strike ballot, the need for cover is of course likely to be foreseeable. On cover generally, the position of the NASUWT, for example, is straightforward:

> *"Instruction 20: Members should refuse to cover for absence"*

Maintained Schools and those academies set up prior to 29 July 2012 are covered by the provisions of the Specified Work Regulations 2012; which require that only qualified teachers may teach classes. Free schools and academies set up after that date are not bound by this requirement; although of course if cover is provided by non-qualified teachers or support staff in the event of a strike, one could imagine this to be a point utilised by the trade union in the inevitable publicity surrounding strike action. If the Head is on strike, they need to delegate their duties to another member of staff in accordance with Guidance. Note, however, that some duties of a Head are non-delegable: see §54 onwards in STPCD.

Disciplinary Action and Trade Union Representatives

Handling disciplinary matters involving trade union representatives is a careful matter. The ACAS code advises the following (para. 30):

> *"Where disciplinary action is being considered against an employee who is a trade union representative the normal disciplinary procedure should be followed. Depending on the circumstances, however, it is advisable to discuss the matter at an early stage with an official employed by the union, after obtaining the employee's agreement."*

It is common also to notify the regional representative prior to the suspension of an employed trade union representative. Of course, care must be taken not to be seen to be subjecting the representative to a detriment on the grounds of trade union activities contrary to s.146 TULR(C)A 1992. It is occasionally argued that suspension of a trade union representative amounts to a detriment on grounds related to union membership or activities. Clearly, this will depend on the circumstances of each individual case. The Tribunal will be concerned with the *purpose* of the act in question (I.e. The suspension), rather than its *effect*: *Gallagher v. The Department of Transport.* The burden of proof will be on the Employer to demonstrate the purpose of the act in question; it is important therefore to be careful before taking the decision to suspend. Further guidance on the decision to suspend can be found in the Chapter on Misconduct and Discipline. Many organisations will have separate sections of their disciplinary policy devoted to disciplinary situations involving trade union representatives, so regard must be had to those where relevant.

The Right to be Accompanied – s.10 Employment Relations Act 1999

S.10 of the Employee Relations Act provides Employees with the right to be accompanied by a work colleague or a trade union representative at a disciplinary or grievance hearing. Should the work colleague or trade union representative be unavailable for the hearing, they have a right to request an adjournment provided the Employee proposes a reasonable alternative time within five working days. If that is the case, the Employer must postpone the hearing to the time proposed. Failure to comply with the provisions of rise to a potential Tribunal claim, for which the award is two weeks pay, subject to the statutory maximum on week's pay.

It is the request to be accompanied which must be reasonable, and *not* the choice of companion. It is difficult to envisage a situation in which a request to be accompanied per se would not be reasonable. In other words, if the Employee makes a request to be accompanied, their choice of companion is irrelevant: they can choose who they like, provided they are either a work colleague or trade union representative. In practice, if an Employee's companion is likely to be a witness or to prejudice the process in some way, organisations will often ask them to provide another choice: though it is not mandatory for them to do so. Practically, it is a good idea to make your organisations policy on this clear.

It is worth noting that the ACAS Code of Practice, suggests some parameters for the reasonableness of companion in this way:

> "*What is reasonable will depend on the circumstances of each individual case. However, it would not normally be reasonable for workers to insist on being accompanied by a companion whose presence would prejudice the hearing nor would it be reasonable for a worker to ask to be accompanied by a companion from a remote geographical location if someone suitable and willing was available on site.*"

As is immediately obvious, this is contrary to the principle set out above, which come directly from case law. Nevertheless, I would recommend using the ACAS guidance above as a normal rule of thumb, whilst bearing in mind that ultimately, it is not for the employer to choose the companion in this way.

Normal practice in the sector is to try to agree proposed dates for such hearings with the Employee and/or their representatives in advance; and whilst that is desirable that can lead to delay, for example, when a specific representative is not available. Since delay in progressing such matters has the real potential to disadvantage both Employer and Employee, Schools should consider being prescriptive as to the timings of hearings; attendance at which, provided they are during normal working hours, can reasonably be regarded as a reasonable management instruction. This is particularly the case given the right to request a postponement. Occasionally Unions will threaten to invoke the postponement provision of s.10, without actually doing so. I would advise taking a hard line (within reasonable parameters) if in receipt of such communication, for the following reasons:

a) It is in neither party's interests for the matter to be unduly delayed;

b) It is the Employee's right to request a postponement, not the Unions (although they can certainly act on the Employee's behalf); and

c) Nothing in the legislation affords the Employee the right to be accompanied by a specific trade union representative, just one that meets the definition of a representative within the Trade Union and Labour Relations (Consolidation) Act 1992.

All the main teaching unions ought to be sufficiently resourced to be able to provide a representative with the relatively generous time periods that most Schools provide when scheduling a disciplinary hearing.

Summary

Trade Union relations remain a key consideration for all working in the education sector. Good trade union relations, and quality representation can be significantly beneficial to Schools; but conversely when relations deteriorate this has a significant impact on the organisation. Although the Trade Union Act 2016 has limited the situations in which strike action can be taken, the power of the unions and the role they play within the sector means that any situation must be handled with reference to the impact on any recognised trade unions. It should always be borne in mind that trade unions have significant resources, and will often fund litigation for their members.

CHAPTER TWELVE
WHISTLEBLOWING

Introduction

In this chapter, we will look at the topic of whistleblowing in the workplace and the regime introduced by the Public Interest Disclosure Act; reviewing what is capable of constituting a protected disclosure; and how for the unwary this can lead to potential claims against School.

Public Interest Disclosures

The concept of making a Public Interest Disclosure, more commonly known as a whistleblowing disclosure, was introduced by the Public Interest Disclosure Act. The provisions for making a protected disclosure are now contained within the Employment Rights Act:

> *"In this Part a "qualifying disclosure" means any disclosure of information which, in the reasonable belief of the worker making the disclosure, is made in the public interest and tends to show one or more of the following—*
>
> *(a) that a criminal offence has been committed, is being committed or is likely to be committed,*
>
> *(b) that a person has failed, is failing or is likely to fail to comply with any legal obligation to which he is subject,*
>
> *(c) that a miscarriage of justice has occurred, is occurring or is likely to occur,*
>
> *(d) that the health or safety of any individual has been, is being or is likely to be endangered,*

(e) *that the environment has been, is being or is likely to be damaged, or*

(f) *that information tending to show any matter falling within any one of the preceding paragraphs has been, is being or is likely to be deliberately concealed."* (S.43B Employment Rights Act 1996).

The Act goes on to prescribe various named people to who the disclosure must be made: an employer is one of them, and it is the employer with whom we are concerned in this chapter.

The first thing to note is that disclosure can be made by a 'worker'; not just an Employee, so this potentially covers a wider ambit of people engaged at School than just pure Employees.

Failure to comply with a legal obligation

Whilst most of the matters which can constitute a qualifying disclosure are straightforward, it is important to note the potentially wide ambit of (b): *"that a person has failed, is failing or is likely to fail to comply with any legal obligation to which he is subject".*

This wording has been taken to include, for example, compliance with a contract of employment: since this is, of course, a legal obligation to which a person is subject. For this reason, a number of claims were brought alleging whistleblowing where a person was also alleging, for example, bullying and harassment: the failure in legal obligation being an alleged failure to abide by the implied contractual term of mutual trust and confidence.

Disclosure itself

There is no specific requirement or standard form for making a disclosure. All that is required is that a worker conveys information to an

Employer regarding any of the matters listed above. This can be done verbally, or in writing: clearly, a worker is more likely to be successful in a claim if they can demonstrate a disclosure made in writing. So, for example, it is not uncommon for a worker to argue that a grievance also constitutes a protected disclosure. However, simply making an allegation is not enough: the disclosure must convey facts.

Public Interest

The disclosure itself must be in the public interest. There is no further definition given within the legislation itself; so we must look to the courts to help us with the definition. In the case of *Chesterton v. Nurmohamed*, an estate agent successfully argued that a failure to pay him a bonus due to an alleged overstating of the running costs of a London office, was in the public interest. In essence, the argument was that the figures were being manipulated for the benefit of the shareholders. This affected both Mr Nurmohamed, as well as 100 other employees; and on these facts, this disclosure was potentially in the public interest.

This is an extreme example, and in Schools cases it is easy to see situations where the disclosure may well be in the public interest: for example, a disclosure regarding improper conduct in the examination process would almost certainly be in the public interest.

Reasonable belief

It is not necessary for the disclosure itself to be factually correct: it is enough that the worker making the disclosure has a reasonable belief that the disclosure is true. This is objectively assessed, and will involve looking at both what the worker actually knew as well as what reasonable person would conclude in the circumstances.

Whistleblowing claims

A person making a protected disclosure is protected in 2 ways: first, from being subjected to a detriment; and secondly, if they are an employee, from being unfairly dismissed.

The meaning of detriment is discussed within the chapter on discrimination: it goes further than 'less favourable treatment', being something an objective person would regard as unfavourable. A detriment claim on these grounds can be brought during the currency of employment.

The protection from unfair dismissal comes in the form of making a dismissal for which the sole or principal reason is the making of a protected disclosure automatically unfair. These claims are not subject to the 'cap' on damages of 52 weeks' pay; and can also lead to claims for injury to feelings, which is discussed in more detail in the chapter on discrimination.

Summary

As can be seen, the situations in which a whistleblowing discourse could arise are wider that may first appear to be the case. Many organisations will have in place a detailed policy as to how the complaints should be dealt with. Note that although occasionally it may be sensible to grant anonymity to the 'whistleblower', this is not a legal requirement (although they cannot be subjected to a detriment). I would suggest the situation on anonymity be reviewed on a case by case basis, and not automatically promised since it may in practice be very difficult to achieve.

CHAPTER THIRTEEN
UNFAIR DISMISSAL

Introduction

In this chapter, we will look at the claim of unfair dismissal. Unfair dismissal is a statuary claim, governed by the provisions of the Employment Rights Act. In provides a right to Employees to bring a claim to an Employment Tribunal to seek reinstatement, re-engagement or (most commonly) compensation in the event of being dismissed unfairly. In this chapter, we will look at the following issues:

- Who has the right to bring a claim;
- The fair reasons for dismissal – and what the Tribunal will look at when examining each reason;
- The potential remedies open to an Employee if they are unfairly dismissed.

Unfair Dismissal – The right to bring a claim

The right to bring a claim for dismissal is open to Employees only; and not, for example, workers, sub-contractors or volunteers. This does in certain circumstances lead to litigation about the relative employment status of individuals; which reinforces the need for Schools to be careful in the designation of those with whom it interacts.

In order to qualify for the right, employees must be continuously employed for a period of 2 years. Note that the provisions of the Modification Order mentioned above to not apply so as to generate service to bring an unfair dismissal claim: it must be 2 years at the School, Academy, or Local Authority as the case may be. However, any service accrued prior to a TUPE transfer (for example, on academisation) will 'count' as continuous service for the purposes of bringing an unfair dismissal claim.

There are also a number of what is described in the legislation as 'automatic' reasons for unfair dismissal, which do not require a period of qualifying service at all. In these cases, regardless of the fairness or otherwise, the law deems the dismissal unfair. The test is focused on looking at what was the sole or principal *reason* for dismissal: if that reason falls within the category listed below, the dismissal will be unfair. The main ones to be aware of in a Schools context are as follows:

1. Dismissal for family related reasons; I.e. As a result of taking or requesting maternity, parental or adoption leave;
2. Whistleblowing;
3. Dismissal for health and safety-related reasons;
4. Dismissal for asserting a statutory right;
5. Trade union membership or activities;
6. Dismissal on the grounds of being a part-time or fixed-term worker/employee;
7. Whistleblowing;
8. Dismissal for exercising the right to request flexible working;
9. Dismissal as a result of a TUPE transfer where the organisation does not have an economic, technical or organisational reason (although note that this type of unfair dismissal claim *does* require 2 years continuous service).

The Fair Reasons for Dismissal

The Employment Rights Act give the following potentially 'fair' reasons for dismissal:

- Conduct;
- Capability (which includes both performance and ill-health);
- Redundancy;
- Statutory illegality;
- Some other Substantial Reason (commonly referred to by the acronym 'SOSR')

Conduct, capability and redundancy are all dealt with in the chapters above. We will look in a little more detail at statutory illegality and SOSR below.

In all circumstances, the Tribunal - which is not entitled to substitute its own view for that of the employer - will look at fairness in the circumstances. This includes looking at the size and administrative resources of the employer. This can work against Schools in some circumstances, with Tribunal judges assuming they have the full backup of the parent local authority, which of course may not necessarily be the case.

Illegality

If the contract of employment is itself illegal, or becomes illegal due to a change in the law then dismissal for that reason will not be unfair. However, the situations in which illegality apply are very limited indeed, and would almost certainly be unlikely to arise in a Schools.

For example, whilst the conviction of a teacher for a criminal offence resulting in them being placed on the barred list and/or being the subject of a prohibition order from the relevant regulatory authority may technically constitute illegality, it is likely that this would also constitute gross misconduct: and I would advise proceeding with a dismissal on this basis, rather than relying on illegality since the burden on the School is easier to satisfy in a Tribunal setting.

Some Other Substantial Reason

The concept of '*Some Other Substantial Reason*', or SOSR as it is more commonly referred to operates as a 'catch-all' provision for dismissals that do not necessarily fall within any of the other categories of fair reasons for dismissal set out within the Employment Rights Act. Whilst it is not possible to give an exhaustive list of situations in which SOSR will apply, common situations include:

- A business reorganisation falling short of redundancy;
- Third-party pressure to dismiss;
- In a safeguarding context, disclosure of relevant information from the authorities

A business reorganisation falling short of redundancy tends to be used mainly in conjunction with a defence to an unfair dismissal claim where the dismissal is on the grounds of redundancy. It is very rare, and probably unadvisable, for a School to proceed simply on this basis, as opposed to labelling it as a pure redundancy during any restructure process.

A dismissal can be fair for SOSR if there is third-party pressure to dismiss. This could come, for example, from a key stakeholder. If this is a potential consideration, it is very important to balance the needs of School against any potential injustice to the employee. Care should be taken to examine the source of the complaint by the third-party and whether it is justifiable, the employee's response to the complaint, as well as looking carefully at what, if any, alternative positions are available for the affected employee.

Safeguarding and Some Other Substantial Reason

A particularly problematic area can arise where a School receives information – potentially unsolicited – that leads to potential safeguarding concerns. This situation arose with OFCOM, the communications watchdog, and a look at the facts of that situation illustrates the points and the approach to take.

In that case, OFCOM were notified that Mr Leach, employed by OFCOM as their International Policy Advisor (Professional Senior Associate) were notified by the Serious and Organised Crime Authority that Mr Leach had been arrested in Cambodia on suspicion of child abuse offences. OFCOM has a statutory duty to have regard to the vulnerability of children. The advice from the Police was that they viewed Mr Leach as continuing to pose a threat to children. As a result of that, OFCOM took the decision, following a disciplinary hearing, to summarily dismiss the Claimant.

In essence, however, the 'fair' reason for the purposes of the Employment Rights Act 1996 was some other substantial reason. In these circumstances, the Court of Appeal agreed that OFCOM did have such reason for the dismissal of the Claimant. The factors that were especially relevant included the public reputation of OFCOM, the credible source of the information presented to OFCOM (the Police), and the efforts taken by OFCOM to balance the needs of the organisation against the potential for injustice to the Employee.

If we contrast that decision with the one reached in *Z v. A* [2013] UKEAT 0203_13_0912, in which the decision of a governing body of a primary school to dismiss a caretaker on the basis of information (again from the police) of an allegation of historical sex abuse was found to be unfair. In that case, the School had demonstrated no sound basis for their conclusion that the Claimant posed a danger to children. The matter was still the subject of police investigation at the time of the dismissal; indeed at the time of the appeal, the Claimant provided a specific date for the conclusion of the police investigation which was only 8 days in the future.

Clearly, therefore, the situation must be approached with some caution. Taken from the OFCOM case, and paraphrasing, I would suggest considering the following steps when dealing with this type of dismissal:

1. The nature of the Respondent and the Claimant's role in it;
2. The nature of the allegations and the efforts made by the Respondent to obtain clarification and confirmation;
3. The response of the Claimant;
4. What alternative courses of action have been reasonably open to the Respondent.

In essence, it is a question of balancing the risk to the Employer as against the potential injustice to the affected Employee. Further guidance is provided in the headnote to the OFCOM case:

> "*an employer to whom a third party discloses information or makes allegations should assess for itself, as far as practicable the reliability of what it has been told, it should check the integrity of the informant body and the safeguards within its internal processes containing the accuracy of the information supplied. It should consider also the likely effect of disclosure and whether there was cogent evidence of a pressing need for disclosure to the employer.*"

Anderson v. Chesterfield High School [2015] is a recent example of the EAT dealing with SOSR in a Schools context. In that case, the Claimant held a role at the School; which ceased upon him becoming Leader of Liverpool City Council. However, the employing authority (Sefton Borough Council) retained him as an employee on the basis that he would be paid the maximum allowed as paid leave to enable employees to hold public office. This equated to approximately £4,500 per annum. The School subsequently became an academy, by which time the Claimant had become the elected Mayor of Liverpool, a role which carried with it an annual allowance to the tune of £80,000. Understandably, the Academy looked to terminate the employment of the Claimant, since the financial sum paid to him provided no benefit to pupils at the School. Although the procedure followed by the School was unfair, the reason – some other substantial reason – was held to be a fair one in the circumstances.

It is also important that the decision maker has some understanding of what is meant by some other substantial reason. Simply applying the moniker 'breakdown in trust and confidence' is unlikely to be enough for a Tribunal to accept: it is important to get behind why the reason is substantial for that particular School; and how it reasonably applies so as to justify the dismissal of the employee. Remember that the decision maker is likely to be cross-examined on this point; so a detailed understanding – which should be evidenced in the dismissal outcome letter – is crucial.

Wherever this situation arises, extreme care should be taken, and professional advice sought.

Constructive Dismissal

Constructive Dismissal, a phrase that is often used without foundation, can lead to a claim for unfair dismissal; provided the employee has the requisite length of service.

An Employee is entitled to bring a claim in circumstances where the employer's conduct is so bad that it entitles the employee to regard the contract of employment as at an end. The classic explanation would be if an Employer failed to pay the Employees – pay being a fundamental term of any employment contract; and any breach of a fundamental term can legitimately lead to a claim for constructive unfair dismissal.

It is difficult to give a fully exhaustive list of circumstances that will lead to a claim for constructive dismissal. What is necessary is for the employer's conduct to amount to a fundamental breach of the contract of employment. The vast majority of constructive dismissal claims rely on a breach of something known as the implied term of 'mutual trust and confidence'.

Mutual trust and confidence – between Employer and Employee – is implied into all employment contracts as a matter of law. If an Employer conducts themselves in a matter calculated, or likely to, breach that term, an Employee can be entitled to treat themselves as constructively dismissed.

This situation commonly arises in response to, e.g. demotions, workplace bullying or harassment, or perceived poor management. Whist it is not a formal pre-requisite to bringing a claim, a Tribunal would normally have expected the Employee to have brought a grievance prior to any resignation: for this reason, it is important that grievances are dealt with promptly and with due care.

It is necessary for the Employee to resign in response to the alleged breach: that does not they have to resign *immediately* – but they must not wait too long. It is generally advisable for an Employer to provide the Employee with the opportunity to reconsider a resignation – commonly referred to as a 'cooling off' period. Whilst this on its own will not defeat a claim for constructive dismissal, it will certainly assist.

From a practical point of view, constructive dismissal is one of the more difficult areas for an Employee to be successful in. This is partly due to the fact that the Tribunal places the burden on the Employee to prove that the Employer's conduct was *so bad* as to entitle them to resign. It can be the case, for example, that the Employer's conduct could be bad: but just not bad enough.

That does not, however, make the claims easy for Employers to defend: constructive dismissal claims will often involve a sequence of allegations, often historical in nature which can require the production of extensive documentation and a large amount of time in Tribunal to determine.

Remedies – reinstatement and re-engagement

In the event of an unfair dismissal claim succeeding, an Employee is entitled to remedy from the Employment Tribunal. The remedies that are available are:

- Reinstatement
- Re-engagement
- Compensation

By far the most common remedy sought is compensation.

Reinstatement involves an order from the Employment Tribunal compelling the Employer to reinstate the Employee in their previous role. Re-engagement is an order compelling the Employe to re-engage the Employee in a comparable role. If so ordered, the Employer will also have to pay loss of earnings from the date of the dismissal to the date of the reinstatement or re-engagement; and a failure to comply with the order can lead to a financial penalty of between 26 – 52 weeks pay.

Unsurprisingly, given the inevitable breakdown in the relationship that results from a dismissal; reinstatement and re-engagement are rarely sought by an Employee, and even more rarely ordered by a Tribunal. When deciding on whether to make such an order, the Tribunal will take into account the wishes of the Employee, whether or not the employee contributed to their dismissal, and how practicable it will be for the Employer to comply with the terms of the order.

If faced with such a possibility, care should be taken to produce evidence to demonstrate the practical difficulties or otherwise the School would face if forced to comply with such an Order; both through documentary and witness evidence.

Remedies – Compensation

As set out above, most Employees will look to recover compensation as a remedy to their unfair dismissal. There are a number of different heads of claim, but the most common (and valuable) ones are the basic award, and compensation for loss of earnings.

Basic Award

A successful tribunal claim for unfair dismissal will in almost all cases attract what is known as a basic award. This is an award based on length of service, and is equivalent to a statutory redundancy payment. It is worked out on gross weekly pay, subject to the statutory cap which currently stands at £525 per week. It is also age-related, with Employees being able to claim 0.5 weeks pay for each year of service under the age of 22, 1 weeks pay for each year of service between 22 – 41, and 1.5 weeks pay for each year of service over the age of 41. The maximum number of years' than can be claimed for is 20.

The calculation is therefore as follows:

A x B x C

Where:

A = length of service
B = age-related multiplier
C = gross weekly pay capped at £525.

So the calculation for a 50 year old employee, with a salary of £50,000 gross and 20 years service would be:

9 x 1.5 x £525 = £7087.50 (i.e. 9 years over the age of 41)

11 x 1 x £525 = £5775

Total - £7087.50 + £5775 = £12862.50.

Compensatory Award – Loss of Earnings

Whilst a number of matters can be claimed for under the Compensatory award; the largest chunk will normally encompass loss of earnings. In a claim for unfair dismissal, this is capped at either 52 weeks pay, or the statutory maximum award (presently £86,444), whichever is the lower. This change arguably does not adequately compensate Employees in the education sector, as it does not account for loss of pension rights; which for final salary schemes (such as the Teachers' Pension Scheme or the Local Government Pension Scheme) will often amount to significantly higher sums of loss than the pure loss of earnings alone. It is perhaps for this reason that an increasing number of claims seek to claim discrimination and/or whistleblowing since a successful claim for these matters removes any cap on compensation.

Note that claims for loss of earnings are worked out on a net loss basis. Loss of Earnings claims can also include claims for future loss of earnings, if the Employee has not found a job at all, or a job that does not pay the same as that previously enjoyed (in which case the award is the difference between the present salary and the previous salary).

However, it is incumbent on the Employee to take steps to mitigate their loss – ordinarily by taking steps to find alternative employment. This can be particularly problematic for teachers, since the timing of a dismissal may raise suspicions with any prospective employer: particularly if it does not coincide with the end of the School term. Similarly, steps to gain alternative employment in teaching may be hindered by an ongoing investigation by a Regulatory body.

Compensatory Award – Other matters

Other matters that can be claimed for include:

- Loss of employee benefits: e.g. gym membership, private healthcare etc.;

- Loss of statutory rights (to compensate for the fact that they will need to accrue a further 2 years' service before attaining the right to claim for unfair dismissal again).

Remedies – Contributory Fault and Polkey

There are 2 main methods that can lead to a reduction; and in some cases, removal, of the compensatory award:

- A reduction for contributory fault; and
- A reduction as a result of the *Polkey* principle (derived from the case of *Polkey v. A E Dayton*).

Contributory Fault

A Tribunal will reduce an Employee's compensation – by up to 100% – if they think that the Employee themselves is in someway to blame for the dismissal. It is necessary for the Employer, in these circumstances, to demonstrate that the Employee is in someway guilty of culpable and/or blameworthy conduct that has led to, or contributed to, the Employer's decision to dismiss. As ever, the situations in which this may arise are many and varied; but such a reduction could be applied where the dismissal is unfair due to some error in procedure, yet the Tribunal is nonetheless satisfied that the Employee was indeed guilty of the misconduct alleged.

Polkey Reduction

A *Polkey* reduction, though often mentioned in the same breath as a contributory fault deduction, is somewhat different. This principle enables the Tribunal to reduce an award of compensation if they are satisfied that 'but for' some flaw in the process, the dismissal would still have happened in any event. For example, it could be the case that a

Tribunal decides a redundancy dismissal is unfair due to a lack of proper consultation on the part of the Employer; yet is still persuaded that notwithstanding the lack of consultation the Employee would still have been dismissed on the grounds of redundancy. In that situation, a Tribunal may for example take the view that the proper consultation would have taken a further, say, 4 weeks, and award the Employee simply 4 weeks loss of earnings as compensation (the employee in question having already received the equivalent of the basic award by virtue of their statutory redundancy payment).

Compensation and the ACAS Code of Practice

By way of a final note, a Tribunal has the power, in the event of a failure *by either party* to comply with the statutory ACAS Code of Practice on Discipline and Grievance to increase or reduce the award payable to reflect the failure.

The maximum amount of reduction and/or increase is 25%. Examples of matters for which a reduction may be applied might be failure by the Employee to comply with the employer's procedure; for example in failing to attend a disciplinary hearing, or not appealing the dismissal. Contrary, an Employer could be penalised for not following their own procedure, or for holding a disciplinary hearing in the absence of the Employee.

Summary

Unfair dismissal is still one of the most regular claims brought to an Employment Tribunal; the prevalence has increased significantly since Tribunal fees were outlawed. However, the key to avoiding such claims is acting reasonably, and in accordance with the relevant policy. Whilst this will not avoid every single claim, it will place any School in the best position to defend a claim if it is brought.

CHAPTER FOURTEEN
EMPLOYMENT TRIBUNALS

Introduction

In this chapter, we will look at the Tribunal process, including the types of claim that can be brought, the early conciliation process, as well as time limits. We will also look at the important aspect of the procedure to be aware of, and the types of hearing and a little on what to expect throughout the claim.

Types of Claim

Employment Tribunals have a wide jurisdiction, and there is a vast number of individual claims that the Tribunal can here (including some Health & Safety matters not directly related to Employment). The most common claims, are, of course, employment related, and cover (this list is non-exhaustive):

- Unfair Dismissal;
- Discrimination in the workplace contrary to the Equality Act;
- Whistleblowing/Protected Disclosure claims;
- Breach of contract claims (subject to a maximum award of £25,000);
- Failure to provide itemised pay slips;
- Failure to provide a statement of main terms and conditions, or an amendment to main terms & conditions (although these claims must be brought in conjunction with other claims);
- Detriment as a result of being a part-time worker;
- Detriment as a result of being a fixed-term worker;

- Failure to provide a redundancy payment;
- Failure to provide (where requested) a written statement of reasons for dismissal.

Early Conciliation & the role of ACAS

Early Conciliation was introduced on the 6th April 2014. The purpose was to aim to resolve employment disputes without having to have recourse to the Employment Tribunal. Administered by ACAS, it is a pre-requisite to bringing a claim: it is not possible to bring a claim without receiving a certificate from ACAS confirming that early conciliation has been undertaken.

Early Conciliation has an effect on time limits – which is dealt with under the time limits section below.

The process is relatively simple; and can be instigated both by the Employer and the Employee, though of course it is normally the Employee that institutes the process. It involves submitting an online form to ACAS, which on receipt will institute the 28 day period of early conciliation. During this period, an ACAS conciliator will contact both parties to ascertain whether there is a possibility of settlement. It is open to either party to refuse to enter into conciliation (indeed, the Employee can state this right at the start); and that will have no bearing whatsoever on the outcome of any future Tribunal claim.

If the conciliator believes a settlement is close, the conciliator can, with the agreement of the parties, extend the period of early conciliation by up to a further 14 days.

Some practical points to note: firstly, it is open to the Employee to state who in the Employer's organisation ACAS should contact. Whilst in a School, you would normally hope this would be the Head or the Business Manager this might not necessarily be the case, so it is important that staff have at least enough awareness of the process to be in a position to alert the Head/Business Manager to a call from ACAS.

Secondly, it is often quite difficult for Schools to reach a settlement at the early conciliation stage; since this does not always produce a paper trail for audit purposes. It is often the case that only once School can see the merits of the claim in front of them (normally through a formal Tribunal claim) that an informed decision about settlement can be made.

Finally, ACAS have a significant workload. This can mean that although there is a 28-day period, they might not be in a position to contact School until quite late in the process. Again, this can make the process difficult. And of course over the summer period, there may not be any facility in School for such calls to be received: and I would advocate some system to be designed as a potential failsafe in this respect, particularly if School think a claim may be likely.

If a settlement is reached, this will normally be through what is known as a COT3 agreement, and will be an end to the matter. All is not lost, however, if a deal is not reached at early conciliation. ACAS have an ongoing duty throughout the currency of any Tribunal claim to resolve the matter through conciliation wherever possible. An ACAS officer will be appointed at the start of any formal Tribunal claim (note this will not normally be the same person who dealt with the early conciliation) and regular contact with them can be maintained. It is not uncommon for claims to settle at a very late stage indeed, quite often literally whilst waiting to go into Tribunal for a final hearing.

Time limits

The Tribunal has relatively short time limits for claims brought before it. In the vast majority of cases, the time limit will be 3 months (the main exception being a claim for a redundancy payment, for which the time limit is 6 months).

Time limits – unfair dismissal

Time runs from the date of the act that forms the substance of the complaint. So, for an unfair dismissal, the time limit is 3 months – less one day – from the date of the dismissal. So a claim for a dismissal that takes place on the 20th July must be brought by no later than the 19th of October. It is the date of dismissal that counts, *not* the date of the final outcome on an appeal. The actual date of dismissal is taken to be the date on which the dismissal decision is communicated to the Employee. Clearly, this is straightforward if the dismissal is communicated verbally to the Employee: however, in a School in which the local authority is the Employer, this is unlikely to be the case, since the Governing Body must notify the local authority, and then it is for the Local Authority to confirm the decision in writing within 14 days.

An example of how this can lead to an unlikely result is given in the case of *Birmingham City Council v. Emery:*

Ms Emery was employed as a teacher at the school under a contract of employment. Her contract of employment provided for termination with two months' notice expiring on the 30th April or with four months' notice expiring on the 31st August but not on any date in between. Because the school was a community school, the local authority was her employer, Regulation 20 provided that if the governing body determined that she should be dismissed, her employment had to be terminated by the authority. On February 28, a meeting of a panel of governors (which was attended by a representative of the local authority) determined that Ms Emery ought to be dismissed. The local authority representative stated that the date of dismissal was the date of the meeting; that she was entitled to contractual notice pay, ending 30th April, and that a letter confirming the dismissal would be sent to her. Whilst the governing body wrote to her on the 28th February, confirming that the local authority would be terminating her contract on notice ending April 30; it was not until the 29th February 29 that the local authority wrote to her formally terminating her employment as of the 30th April. Ms Emery did not receive the letter until the 1st March. In the employment tribunal , the judge concluded that the letter was one day too late to give her the notice to which she was contractually entitled (under the Burgundy Book) and awarded her a further four months' pay.

The Courts have continually held that when written notice is given, the correct date is not the date of the letter, but the date the Employee reads the letter. As a further example, the case of *Haywood v. Newcastle upon Tyne [2017]* illustrates the point. In that case, the Employee was sent a letter by recorded delivery on the 20th April: notifying her that she was dismissed by reason of redundancy and providing 12 weeks-notice. At the time, she was on holiday; and in the event she did not read the letter until the 27th April. At issue was the actual date of dismissal: specifically whether this was before or after the Employee's 50th birthday, which had a bearing on her pension entitlement. The Court agreed that the contents of the letter had to be communicated to the Employee before it took effect: and in this case that was the 27th April, so that the employment was not terminated until after the Employee's 50th birthday.

A claim can be brought out of time, but only if:

a) It was not 'reasonably practicable' for the Employee to bring the claim in time; and

b) The Employee has filed the claim in a reasonable timescale once it has become 'reasonably practicable' to bring the claim.

This is a very high burden, and will depend on compelling evidence from the Employee as to why it was not reasonably practicable. Ignorance of the law, or one's rights, will not be enough.

Time limits – Discrimination

Again, the time limit in a discrimination claim runs from the date of the act complained of. However, the situation is often more complex in a discrimination complaint, since there may be a number of different alleged acts of discrimination, which would potentially carry their own individual time limits. However, providing an employee can demonstrate that the acts of discrimination, if proven, would constitute a series of continuing acts, the Tribunal will take the date of the last act of discrimination as the date from which time will run.

Furthermore, the Tribunal has a wider discretion in discrimination claims to accept them out of time; since the test is not one of reasonable practicability, but rather involves looking at whether it would be 'just and equitable' to accept the claim out of time. This can mean, therefore, that in a claim for both unfair dismissal and discrimination, the Tribunal might reject the claim of unfair dismissal as being out of time, but agree to hear the claim of discrimination.

Time Limits – Early Conciliation

Early Conciliation has made the time limits a little more complicated. The process of early conciliation places a 'stop' on the time-limit clock in all cases where employment has already terminated. The clock is stopped for the duration of the early conciliation; which can of course be less than the maximum 28 days. The provisions apply to give potential Claimants up to an extra month to bring their claim. So, using the example date above:

- Dismissal – 20th July
- Normal time limit – 19th October
- Early Conciliation – 1st - 28th September
- New time limit – 28th October

If the time limit would expire during the Early Conciliation period, the time limit is extended so to be within one month of the date of early conciliation ending. So:

- Dismissal – 20th July

- Normal time limit – 19^{th}October
- Early Conciliation – 18th to 25th October
- New time limit – 25th November

The practical effect of this for Schools is to bear in mind that claims do now take longer to come to light, as the time limit can now be up to 4 months, as opposed to the 3 month period that many will have been used to.

Employment Tribunal Procedure

Although Tribunals were (and are) set up as a relatively informal process by which workplace disputes could be resolved, there are now considerably detailed procedural rules that govern the Tribunal process. It is beyond the scope of this work to list those in detail, but it is useful to look at some of the powers of the Tribunal in a procedural context.

Importantly, a Tribunal can compel a party (and, in some cases, a non-party) to the claim to disclose documents relevant to the case. These can be both actual (i.e. Written down) documents, and electronic documents. In a Schools case, the Tribunal will normally be happy for the identity of any children to be redacted. The Tribunal can issue a fine of up to £1,000 for failure to comply with their orders.

A Tribunal can also order a claim to be heard in private; although this is extremely rare, and limited to cases involving national security, sexual misconduct, or the disclosure of sensitive medical information in a disability case.

A Tribunal can also issue a witness summons compelling a witness to attend Tribunal and give evidence: although, again, this is quite rare.

The normal principle in a Tribunal is that each party will be responsible for their own legal (or other) costs. The exception is if the Tribunal is satisfied that either the case itself, or the manner in which it has been conducted is vexatious, misconceived or an abuse of process. Costs are awarded only rarely; though they are threatened by opposing litigants fairly regularly.

Although it is impossible to set out the normal process of a Tribunal claim (since they all differ), for a straightforward unfair dismissal claim, the timetable might look like this (with hypothetical dates):

- ET1 issued – 1st August
- ET3 deadline – 28th August
- Claimant ordered to produce a Schedule of Loss – 28th August
- Both parties to disclose documents on which they seek to rely – 28th September
- The Respondent to produce the trial bundle – 28th October
- Witness statements to be exchanged – 28th November
- Final Hearing – 2nd January

The target for the Tribunals is for cases to be heard within 26 weeks of the claim being issued.

To give more detail on some of the points above: The ET1 Form is the form the Claimant (I.e. The Employee) must use to issue the claim. The Respondent (I.e. The Employer) must respond using the ET3 Form. This is provided to the Respondent with a pack sent to the Respondent initially. This contains the notice of claim informing them of the claim, a copy of the ET1 Form, a blank ET3 form to complete, a notice of the hearing date, and a timetable for bringing the case to a hearing.

A Schedule of Loss is a statement from the Claimant setting out the damages or other remedy they seek to claim from the Respondent. In some cases, a Respondent may wish to prepare a counter-schedule: this is particularly useful if the Respondent contends that the figures given by the Claimant are incorrect.

The duty to disclose documents extends to all documents which are relevant to the case *whether or not* they support that party's case. Disclosure should be done in accordance with the Tribunal's timetable: parties cannot be ambushed by the production of evidence at the last minute; and the Tribunal can refuse to take any evidence not disclosed in the proper way into account.

The trial bundle is simply an indexed, paginated file of the documents that the Tribunal will need to see in order to decide the case. The Respondent is normally asked to produce this since they generally have greater resources available than the Claimant.

Witness statements ought to be a full statement of the evidence that any witness wishes to give the Tribunal. They should be produced in a logical, chronological manner, referring by page number to any relevant documentation.

Employment Tribunal Hearings

The Tribunal has 2 main types of hearing: a Preliminary Hearing, and a Final Hearing.

Preliminary Hearings

As the name suggests, these hearings take place in advance of the final hearing; and are almost always heard by an Employment Judge sitting alone. If both parties are legally represented, these hearings can take place by telephone to save the cost and expense of the parties physically attending the Tribunal.

They are aimed at either getting the case ready for the final hearing; or on dealing with a discrete issue: for example, whether a case has been presented out of time. It is common in discrimination cases for a preliminary hearing to be listed at the outset in order to clarify the issues to be decided in the case.

Final Hearing

Final hearings (sometimes referred to as the trial) are the final determination on the issues in the case. For the majority of cases, they are now heard by an Employment Judge sitting alone. An Employment Judge is by background either a solicitor or barrister of at least 5 years' experience – though this is normally more – with a background and expertise in employment law. In discrimination cases, the case will be heard by a full panel, consisting of an Employment Judge together with 2 lay members – one from an employee background (e.g. a trade union representative), and one from an employer background. Together they all decide on the outcome of the case, with direction from the Judge as to law.

Final Hearings can be listed for any amount of time, the most common being between 1 and 5 days; though hearings lasting much longer are not unheard of. The Tribunal will not have seen any of the documents relating to the case, and so after a brief set of introductions, the Tribunal will normally take reading time, during which they will read the witness statements and all relevant documents they are referred to. The standard day in Tribunal runs from 10–1, and 2–4 with an hour for lunch. Tribunals aim to give a final outcome, including assessing what (if any) compensation is due within the time allotted for hearing the case. If this is not possible, the Tribunal may give a 'reserved judgment', which involves the Tribunal communicating the outcome in writing to the parties after the end of the hearing. If this is the case, the Tribunal will normally try to give a timescale for this.

Appeals

If either party is dissatisfied with the Tribunal's judgment, they have the right to either ask the Tribunal to reconsider their decision; or to lodge a formal appeal with the Employment Appeals Tribunal. There are strict time limits and requirements to be aware of: these are beyond the scope of this work.

An appeal can only be lodged if the party believes that Tribunal has got the law wrong; or if they can show that the Tribunal has made a perverse finding of fact. That is more than simply disagreeing with the Tribunals findings; the simplest way of explaining this would be on reading the judgment to say "Oh my Gosh, that must be wrong". Unsurprisingly, this ground of appeal rarely succeeds. One of the most common grounds of appeal is to argue that the Tribunal has substituted their view for that of a reasonable employer: again, this rarely succeeds.

Nor is the Employment Appeal Tribunal necessarily the end of the line. There lies a further route of appeal from the Employment Appeal Tribunal to the Court of Appeal, and from there to the Supreme Court – although both the Court of Appeal and the Supreme Court will normally only agree to hear any appeal if there is some wider public importance to the point being argued.

Summary

The Employment Tribunal process can at first seem daunting, and complicated. However, the system is designed to be as user-friendly as possible; and nearly all Employment Judges are incredibly good (and well-versed) at providing assistance to unrepresented litigants where necessary. I would encourage any person involved in managing staff within School to attend a Tribunal hearing – they are public hearings, and any member of the public can attend – as this will give an invaluable insight into the process.

CHAPTER FIFTEEN
RESOLVING DISPUTES

Introduction

In this chapter, we will look at the various methods Schools can use for resolving workplace disputes, and the things to be aware of when considering those procedures. It should always be remembered that the vast majority of workplace disputes can (and should) be resolved informally wherever possible: this chapter looks at the options when that has proved impossible.

Grievances

Often the first indicator of any workplace dispute, the grievance, in its simplest form, is complaint regarding some aspect of work. Since at one time it was a pre-requisite to raise a formal grievance to be able to lodge a Tribunal claim, there has been a large amount of case law as to what actually constitutes a grievance in a legal sense, and the definition has been drawn quite wide: including, for example, letters from solicitors and GPs.

Nearly all Schools will have a grievance policy in place, setting out the mechanism for formally raising a grievance. Sometimes there will also be a separate policy dealing with bullying and harassment complaints, and with whistleblowing complaints: though this is not a legal requirement.

STPCD requires all maintained Schools to have a grievance policy in place that complies with the provisions of the ACAS Code of Practice on Discipline and Grievance in the workplace.

If a grievance is raised by an employee, it sensible to meet with the employee in question to understand the issue in detail, and set out the

Schools proposed steps for dealing with the grievance. Similarly, it is also important to understand from the Employee what resolution they are looking for – although, of course, not every proposed resolution will be possible.

A normal procedure will involve meeting with the employee, interviewing any relevant witnesses, and producing a report and a proposed outcome to the grievance: stating clearly whether or not the grievance is upheld or not. The procedure ought also to have a right of appeal for the affected employee.

Problems occur when a grievance is raised during the currency of a disciplinary investigation against the grieving employee. It is important to be clear in both the disciplinary and grievance policy as to what will happen in this situation. Some organisations will have a rule that a grievance cannot be raised about the fact of the disciplinary investigation. It is, furthermore, legally permissible to run a disciplinary process and a grievance process concurrently: although this can be practically difficult.

Another point to consider carefully is what happens to the person raising the grievance whilst it is being investigated: particularly if, for example, they are raising a grievance against their direct line manager. Care needs to be taken not to subject them to a detriment as a result of raising the grievance; not least as this could give rise to a further complaint. If possible, this question should be addressed both at the outset of the process – seeking agreement with the Employee – and consistently reviewed throughout the process.

As many Schools will appoint governors to either investigate or to decide on the grievance (depending on how serious the complaint is), formal training should be provided to those governors so they are clear about their remit and responsibilities. I would also suggest careful scheduling of the timings of the process and any hearing at the outset: since an overly lengthy process is likely to be criticised in the event of a Tribunal claim, as well as being detrimental to the Employee and the School. In a particularly serious grievance, thought should be given as to whether the appointment of an external investigator would be sensible to ensure objectivity and that the grievance is dealt with in a timely fashion.

Protected Conversations

Protected conversations, introduced into the Employment Rights Act in 2013, provide a mechanism for an Employer to have an 'off the record' discussion with an employee regarding various issues (most commonly performance and/or disciplinary issues), normally with a view to resolving the issues without recourse to more formal matters, for example, a formal disciplinary hearing. The resolution this normally leads to is an agreed settlement agreement terminating the employment by means of mutual consent.

Provided certain conditions are met and adhered to, the conversation cannot be referred to in any subsequent tribunal or court matters. In that sense, they are akin to 'without prejudice' communications: yet, crucially, there does not need to be an existing dispute between the parties for the conversation to remain protected.

ACAS has produced a statutory guide on settlement agreements; this contains a useful piece of standard correspondence that can be tailored to the relevant situation. Key points to note are as follows:

1. Protected conversations ought not to be utilised in situations where there is likely to be an equality act complaint (i.e. One of discrimination), or one that could lead to a potential complaint of automatic unfair dismissal – e.g. a whistleblowing complaint;

2. If there is any improper conduct on the part of either party, the conversation will lose its protection;

3. Although there is no statutory obligation for an employee to be accompanied to such a conversation, it may be advisable to provide the employee with accompaniment as an option at least

at the outset of the meeting if a formal invitation has not been sent prior;

4. As the Employer, make sure you are accompanied to avoid any suggestion of impropriety;
5. The Employee has 10 calendar days to consider any offer made – confirm the offer in writing immediately (you may wish to pre-prepare this correspondence in advance, and it can serve as a useful aide memoire for the conversation itself);
6. Consider whether to allow the Employee some (paid) time off to consider the offer – especially if the situation is likely to come as a shock.

Whilst by no means a catch-all solution, protected conversations are a useful management tool. They are becoming increasingly common in commercial organisations, although they are less prevalent in the education sector. Be wary, though, of using a protected conversation in every single situation: as this can lead to a lack of trust or a feeling of uncertainty amongst staff members; as well as a means of 'buying out' tricky problems in situations where careful staff management can produce a better result: for example, retaining the services of a normally loyal and hard-working, yet temporarily disaffected employee. My advice would be to utilise protected conversations where a quick outcome is needed – it is certainly quicker than a drawn-out performance management process – or where there is a breakdown in the relationship without there being necessarily a clear example of misconduct.

One final point to be aware of – a protected conversation will almost never be appropriate where there is an alleged safeguarding breach. The DfE Guidance 'Keeping Children Safe in Education' advocates against reaching negotiated settlement in such situations; and no settlement agreement will avoid the need either to make a safeguarding disclosure to the local authority; or a referral to the Teachers Regulation Authority when the relevant threshold is met.

Settlement Agreements

Settlement agreements are one of only two lawful methods of an Employee waiving their statutory rights (the other one being an agreement reached via ACAS, commonly referred to as a 'COT3' agreement). They are often – though not exclusively – reached as a result of a protected conversation. In order to be a valid settlement agreement, it is necessary for an Employee to receive independent legal advice on the contents of the agreement prior to signature. Only the following classes of people can provide the advice:

- A qualified solicitor;
- A qualified barrister; or
- A trade union officer certified by the trade union as being competent to provide the advice.

For the vast majority of cases, it will be a solicitor that provides the advice. It is the job of the legal adviser to ensure that the employee understands the terms of the settlement agreement, and the implications of signing the agreement. It is normal for the Employer to make at least a contribution towards the costs of that legal advice. The fees for this vary, although it is commonly between £250 – £500 plus VAT. Also note the advisor should be independent: so it will not be appropriate for any legal advisor advising School to provide the advice to the Employee in question.

A settlement agreement will normally serve to settle all and any outstanding potential employment-related claims against the employer. The only claims that an Employee cannot waive are for accrued pension rights and for a personal injury of which they are not presently aware (e.g. for asbestosis, which may not manifest itself until some years after the end of the employment). If there is an ongoing personal injury claim, it is normal for this to be expressly excluded from the terms of any settlement agreement.

It is also common for settlement agreements to contain a confidentiality provision, keeping the terms of the settlement agreement confidential (and sometimes the facts leading up to the agreement as well). Care should be taken when entering into these agreements, particularly if the allegations surround safeguarding and/or sexual harassment claims. No confidentiality provision will prevent an Employee making a whistleblowing disclosure; and any agreement that precludes the right of the Employer to make a referral (where appropriate) to the TRA is likely to be void; as well as leaving the School open to potentially committing a criminal offence by the fact of failing to make the relevant disclosure.

Mediation

Mediation is a process aimed at resolving disputes between parties. It will often involve both parties coming together, under an appointed mediator, to talk through the issues that have arisen and to seek a resolution wherever possible.

Though there is no strict requirement to attempt mediation prior to the institution of an Employment Tribunal claim, it should be considered, and can provide a workable solution to workplace disputes even in the most difficult scenarios. Schools can call on the services of ACAS for this purpose, or appoint a professional mediator.

Thought should be given when arranging a mediation to the venue: for example, School is unlikely to be appropriate. Ideally 3 rooms ought to be available – a room for any plenary session, as well as a room for each party. School needs to ensure that those attending for their part have sufficient authority to agree to any proposed resolution.

In certain circumstances, during an Employment Tribunal case, the Tribunal will offer judicial mediation. This will involve an Employment Tribunal Judge acting as a mediator with a view to attempting to resolve the proceedings. Anything said in any such mediation will not be disclosed in the future case, and the Judge acting as mediator will not be appointed to hear any final hearing. For mediation to be offered, the

Tribunal must be satisfied there is a realistic prospect of a resolution being achieved. It is also only offered in those cases that are listed for more than 3 days; and takes place in the Tribunal building.

Many mediations can run quite late: but do not be tempted to agree outline terms with a view to finalising matters at some future point. If possible the whole agreement should be sealed on the day, since it is very often the case that the effect of the mediation can diminish once parties have left the room.

Summary

As can be seen, there are various methods of resolving workplace disputes, and not all of them will lead to an end to the employment relationship. However, this does inevitably occur. It is important, in my view, not to be over-reliant on settlement agreements, as this can lead to more Employees trying to argue for these in circumstances where they are not necessarily justified.

CHAPTER SIXTEEN USEFUL SOURCES OF INFORMATION

I set out here my 'go to' sources of information when advising in the sector; particularly the web or other resources that I and my team utilise on a daily basis:

ACAS Code of Practice on Settlement Agreements:
http://www.acas.org.uk/media/pdf/f/k/11287_CoP4_Settlement_Agreements_v1_0_Accessible.pdf

ACAS Code of Practice on Discipline and Grievance in the Workplace:
https://beta.acas.org.uk/code-of-practice-on-disciplinary-and-grievance-procedures

STPCD – updated annually – available at
https://assets.publishing.service.gov.uk/government/uploads/system/uploads/attachment_data/file/832634/School_teachers_pay_and_conditions_2019.pdf

LGPS issues – the current version is available at:
http://www.lgpsregs.org
This provides an easily searchable version of the current regulations; access to the old regulations, as well as relevant guidance.

Pension loss compensation Guidelines –
https://www.judiciary.gov.uk/wp-content/uploads/2013/08/presidential-guidance-pension-loss-20170810.pdf
– admittedly, maybe not a daily used resource).

DFE Guidance – *"Keeping Children Safe in Education"*:
https://www.gov.uk/government/uploads/system/uploads/attachment_data/file/550511/Keeping_children_safe_in_education.pdf

Teachers' Standards – one page overview – https://www.gov.uk/government/uploads/system/uploads/attachment_data/file/665522/Teachers_standard_information.pdf

Disqualification under the Childcare Act 2006 – statutory guidance – https://www.gov.uk/government/uploads/system/uploads/attachment_data/file/528473/Disqualification_under_the_childcare_act_June2016.pdf

DFE Guidance - *"Advice on trade union facility time in schools"* – https://www.gov.uk/government/uploads/system/uploads/attachment_data/file/410276/advice_on_trade_union_facility_time_in_schools_090315.pdf

NASUWT Guidance – *"National Action Short of Strike Action"*: https://www.nasuwt.org.uk/uploads/assets/uploaded/b7ec630c-edcc-4b29-b449c86481bb60cd.pdf

NUT Guidance – https://www.teachers.org.uk/files/instructions-for-action-short-of-strike-action.pdf

DFE Guidance – *"Handling Strike Action in Schools"* – https://www.gov.uk/government/uploads/system/uploads/attachment_data/file/553757/advice_on_handling_strike_action_update_September_2016.pdf

TRA Guidance – *"Teacher Misconduct: The prohibition of teachers"* – https://www.gov.uk/government/uploads/system/uploads/attachment_data/file/495028/Teacher_Misconduct_The_Prohibition_of_Teachers_advice_updated_26_Jan_2016.pdf

MORE BOOKS BY LAW BRIEF PUBLISHING

A selection of our other titles available now:-

'Ellis on Credit Hire – Sixth Edition' by Aidan Ellis & Tim Kevan
'Tackling Disclosure in the Criminal Courts – A Practitioner's Guide' by Narita Bahra QC & Don Ramble
'A Practical Guide to TOLATA Claims' by Greg Williams
'Artificial Intelligence – The Practical Legal Issues' by John Buyers
'A Practical Guide to Prison Injury Claims' by Malcolm Johnson
'A Practical Guide to Hackney Carriage Licensing in London' by Stuart Jessop
'A Practical Guide to Advising Clients at the Police Station' by Colin Stephen McKeown-Beaumont
'A Practical Guide to Antisocial Behaviour Injunctions' by Iain Wightwick
'Practical Mediation: A Guide for Mediators, Advocates, Advisers, Lawyers, and Students in Civil, Commercial, Business, Property, Workplace, and Employment Cases' by Jonathan Dingle with John Sephton
'Planning Obligations Demystified: A Practical Guide to Planning Obligations and Section 106 Agreements' by Bob Mc Geady & Meyric Lewis
'A Practical Guide to Crofting Law' by Brian Inkster
'A Practical Guide to Spousal Maintenance' by Liz Cowell
'A Practical Guide to the Law of Domain Names and Cybersquatting' by Andrew Clemson
'A Practical Guide to the Law of Gender Pay Gap Reporting' by Harini Iyengar
'A Practical Guide to the Rights of Grandparents in Children Proceedings' by Stuart Barlow
'NHS Whistleblowing and the Law' by Joseph England
'Employment Law and the Gig Economy' by Nigel Mackay & Annie Powell
'A Practical Guide to the General Data Protection Regulation (GDPR)' by Keith Markham

'A Practical Guide to Noise Induced Hearing Loss (NIHL) Claims' by Andrew Mckie, Ian Skeate, Gareth McAloon
'An Introduction to Beauty Negligence Claims – A Practical Guide for the Personal Injury Practitioner' by Greg Almond
'Intercompany Agreements for Transfer Pricing Compliance' by Paul Sutton
'Zen and the Art of Mediation' by Martin Plowman
'A Practical Guide to the SRA Principles, Individual and Law Firm Codes of Conduct 2019 – What Every Law Firm Needs to Know' by Paul Bennett
'A Practical Guide to Licensing Law for Commercial Property Lawyers' by Niall McCann & Richard Williams
'A Practical Guide to Adoption for Family Lawyers' by Graham Pegg
'Essential Motor Finance Law for the Busy Practitioner' by Richard Humphreys
'A Practical Guide to Industrial Disease Claims' by Andrew Mckie & Ian Skeate
'A Practical Guide to the Law of Armed Conflict' by Jo Morris & Libby Anderson
'A Practical Guide to Redundancy' by Philip Hyland
'A Practical Guide to Vicarious Liability' by Mariel Irvine
'A Practical Guide to Claims Arising from Delays in Diagnosing Cancer' by Bella Webb
'A Practical Guide to Applications for Landlord's Consent and Variation of Leases' by Mark Shelton
'A Practical Guide to Relief from Sanctions Post-Mitchell and Denton' by Peter Causton
'Butler's Equine Tax Planning: 2nd Edition' by Julie Butler
'A Practical Guide to Equity Release for Advisors' by Paul Sams
'A Practical Guide to Unlawful Eviction and Harassment' by Stephanie Lovegrove
'A Practical Guide to the Law Relating to Food' by Ian Thomas
'A Practical Guide to the Ending of Assured Shorthold Tenancies' by Elizabeth Dwomoh
'A Practical Guide to Financial Services Claims' by Chris Hegarty
'The Law of Houses in Multiple Occupation: A Practical Guide to HMO Proceedings' by Julian Hunt
'A Practical Guide to Unlawful Eviction and Harassment' by Stephanie Lovegrove

'A Practical Guide to Solicitor and Client Costs' by Robin Dunne
'A Practical Guide to Wrongful Conception, Wrongful Birth and Wrongful Life Claims' by Rebecca Greenstreet
'Occupiers, Highways and Defective Premises Claims: A Practical Guide Post-Jackson – 2nd Edition' by Andrew Mckie
'A Practical Guide to Financial Ombudsman Service Claims' by Adam Temple & Robert Scrivenor
'A Practical Guide to the Law of Enfranchisement and Lease Extension' by Paul Sams
'A Practical Guide to Marketing for Lawyers – 2nd Edition' by Catherine Bailey & Jennet Ingram
'A Practical Guide to Advising Schools on Employment Law' by Jonathan Holden
'Certificates of Lawful Use and Development: A Guide to Making and Determining Applications' by Bob Mc Geady & Meyric Lewis
'A Practical Guide to the Law of Dilapidations' by Mark Shelton
'A Guide to Consent in Clinical Negligence Post-Montgomery' by Lauren Sutherland QC
'A Practical Guide to Running Housing Disrepair and Cavity Wall Claims: 2nd Edition' by Andrew Mckie & Ian Skeate
'A Practical Guide to Digital and Social Media Law for Lawyers' by Sherree Westell
'A Practical Guide to Holiday Sickness Claims – 2nd Edition' by Andrew Mckie & Ian Skeate
'A Practical Guide to Elderly Law' by Justin Patten
'Arguments and Tactics for Personal Injury and Clinical Negligence Claims' by Dorian Williams
'A Practical Guide to QOCS and Fundamental Dishonesty' by James Bentley
'A Practical Guide to Drone Law' by Rufus Ballaster, Andrew Firman, Eleanor Clot
'A Practical Guide to Compliance for Personal Injury Firms Working With Claims Management Companies' by Paul Bennett
'A Practical Guide to the Landlord and Tenant Act 1954: Commercial Tenancies' by Richard Hayes & David Sawtell
'A Practical Guide to Psychiatric Claims in Personal Injury' by Liam Ryan
'A Practical Guide to Dog Law for Owners and Others' by Andrea Pitt

'RTA Allegations of Fraud in a Post-Jackson Era: The Handbook – 2nd Edition' by Andrew Mckie
'RTA Personal Injury Claims: A Practical Guide Post-Jackson' by Andrew Mckie
'On Experts: CPR35 for Lawyers and Experts' by David Boyle
'An Introduction to Personal Injury Law' by David Boyle
'A Practical Guide to Claims Arising From Accidents Abroad and Travel Claims' by Andrew Mckie & Ian Skeate
'A Practical Guide to Chronic Pain Claims' by Pankaj Madan
'A Practical Guide to Claims Arising from Fatal Accidents' by James Patience
'A Practical Approach to Clinical Negligence Post-Jackson' by Geoffrey Simpson-Scott
'Employers' Liability Claims: A Practical Guide Post-Jackson' by Andrew Mckie
'A Practical Guide to Subtle Brain Injury Claims' by Pankaj Madan
'A Practical Guide to Costs in Personal Injury Cases' by Matthew Hoe
'The No Nonsense Solicitors' Practice: A Guide To Running Your Firm' by Bettina Brueggemann
'The Queen's Counsel Lawyer's Omnibus: 20 Years of Cartoons from The Times 1993-2013' by Alex Steuart Williams

www.ingramcontent.com/pod-product-compliance
Lightning Source LLC
LaVergne TN
LVHW021037011026
849160LV00009BA/674